Not My Boy!

Not My Boy!

*A Father, a Son,
and One Family's
Journey with Autism*

RODNEY PEETE
with DANELLE MORTON

HYPERION
New York

Note to Reader: This book represents our family's personal
story and our specific experiences with members of the
medical and educational community in dealing with our son
who is on the autism spectrum. The book is not intended to
substitute for an individual's medical, psychological, or
educational treatment. It is not the equivalent of, nor is it
intended as a replacement for, any professionally supervised
treatment. All matters concerning your health or that of a
family member require specific analysis and medical
treatment and are not the purview of this book. The author
and publisher disclaim any liability arising directly or
indirectly from use of this book.
All url addresses that appear in the appendix are up to date
as of the date of the initial printing of the book.

Copyright © 2010 HollyRod Entertainment

All rights reserved. No part of this book may be used or repro-
duced in any manner whatsoever without the written permission
of the Publisher. Printed in the United States of America.
For information address Hyperion, 114 Fifth Avenue,
New York, New York, 10011.

Library of Congress Cataloging-in-Publication Data
has been applied for.

ISBN 978-1-4013-2361-5

Hyperion books are available for special promotions and pre-
miums. For details contact the HarperCollins Special Markets
Department in the New York office at 212-207-7528, fax
212-207-7222, or e-mail spsales@harpercollins.com.

Design by Nicola Ferguson

FIRST EDITION

10 9 8 7 6 5 4 3 2 1

SUSTAINABLE FORESTRY INITIATIVE
Certified Fiber Sourcing
www.sfiprogram.org

THIS LABEL APPLIES TO TEXT STOCK

We try to produce the most beautiful books possible,
and we are also extremely concerned about the impact
of our manufacturing process on the forests of the world
and the environment as a whole. Accordingly, we've made sure
that all of the paper we use has been certified as coming from
forests that are managed to ensure the protection of the
people and wildlife dependent upon them.

This book is dedicated to my father, Willie Peete, Jr., for being a consistent example of honesty, integrity, and responsibility. You walk the walk, Dad. Thank you for showing me what it takes to be a good man and a good father.

To my wonderful mother, Edna Peete. I love you, Mom.

To my beautiful wife, Holly, and my four incredible children: R.J., Ryan, Robinson, and Roman. You are, and always will be, my inspiration.

To every father out there who loves his son, would do anything for him, and needs a little guidance, this book is for you.

CONTENTS

CONTENTS

ACKNOWLEDGMENTS

I want to thank all the people who shared their stories to help make this book possible: Chris Brancato, Mike Sherrard, Manuel Munguia, Khari Lee, Francisco Fernandez, Erik Linthorst, and Mike Fields.

Also thanks to Dr. Jay Gordon, for his sage medical advice that helped our son and so many other children; Phillip Hain, for his inspiring service to families with autism through his work with Autism Speaks in Los Angeles; Sharon Lowrey, for her unconditional dedication and for welcoming my son with open arms; Dr. Jeff Jacobs; Deanna Staake, for her compassion; Julie Kern and Ken North, for pushing R.J. in school and getting the most out of him; Mark Kretzmann, for believing in R.J. and his goals, and also for getting him on track at UCLA lab school; Tim Lee, for continuing RJ's development, for being tough but fair with him—you are not only his teacher, but a friend he can count on; Principal Jim Kennedy and the faculty and staff at UCLA lab school, for understanding R.J.'s needs; all the faculty and staff at Smart Start; Wilma McDonald, for being our eyes and ears when we are not around and loving our kids like they're hers; Marta Cuellar, for helping when we need her; Max Robinson and James and Sulana Robinson, the big cousins, for always having R.J.'s back; Reeco and Giselle Peete, the little cousins, who give nothing but love; Rebeca Peete, for caring and understanding; Aichi Ali, for all the love; Dolores Robinson, for being there whenever we need her and understanding who each of our kids are and what they need; Matt Robinson, for being a fun uncle and believing in R.J.; Skip Peete, for being a great uncle to the kids and allowing me to tag along with him when we were growing up—you made me better: thank you and I love you; Edna and Willie Peete, for showing me what true love is and teaching me how to work for what I want, and for showing me that marriage is a journey and you have to work at it—I love you; Ryan Elizabeth Peete, you are beautiful and you show us every day what family is all about—I'm so proud of you; Robinson James Peete, you are a fantastic son and thank you for never judging your brother R.J. and for keeping him engaged since the day you were born; Roman Matthew Peete, for always making R.J. answer your questions—you stimulate him like only the youngest of four can do. Rodney Jackson Peete—thank you for being my inspiration: you understand who you are and you are not afraid to embrace and conquer your fears. You are my hero. And thanks to my wife, Holly, for fourteen-plus years of marriage. You helped me fight when it seemed I forgot how. Thank you for your incredible instincts. You never gave up on me. You are my rock and I will always love you.

Not My Boy!

PROLOGUE

The silken burn of an eighteen-year-old Macallan single malt scotch lingered on the edge of my lips before sliding down my throat. My whole body began to glow from the heat of that first sip. As I felt it enter my bloodstream, I knew that I could forget my problems for a while. I hadn't been a hard liquor drinker before my son was diagnosed as being on the autistic spectrum. But that summer after the diagnosis, I began to understand that there's nothing hard about a good scotch. When I was able to enjoy a nice Montecristo #2 with my Macallan, I felt as if I'd claimed a piece of heaven on earth.

My favorite retreat was a private lounge called the Grand Havana Room. It was in the middle of Beverly Hills, but it was a place that felt far removed from it all.

Members entered the lounge through a private elevator in a protected corner of the public restaurant downstairs. This was a sanctuary for the members. There were no crowds and there was no hassle. The staff in the members' lounge knew the regulars by name and knew exactly what they liked. When I arrived, I'd be escorted to the huge humidor that stood at the center of the main room, and by the time I had my Monte in hand, my scotch was already waiting for me on the table by my favorite chair.

Stretched out in the soft leather club chair, it seemed as though no troubles could touch me. I gazed through the two-story-tall windows to a sweeping view of the Hollywood Hills, enjoying the smell of cedar and fine tobacco and the rhythm of my ritual.

When R.J. was diagnosed in 2000, I was grateful that I was playing for the Oakland Raiders because I could come home more often than I'd been able to in the past. I told myself that I was racing home because I wanted to be helpful to my family, but the truth was that I wasn't much help. My wife, Holly, and I couldn't agree on much about R.J. back then. I wanted to be there for my family, but I spent my precious evenings in my favorite chair at the Grand Havana instead of with them. Later, flushed with the success of a good season with the Raiders, the cigars and scotch would be flowing. I convinced myself that the Monte 2 and Macallan was Daddy time. Think of that. Daddy time spent far away from the kids.

I would usually go to the lounge by myself, but other times I'd meet friends there. We never talked about how my boy was struggling. Maybe this was because I wanted to escape the feelings that were killing me inside; maybe I believed my friends couldn't relate; maybe I didn't know how to talk about it. Mostly, I was just scared.

Holly would often call me while I was at the club. When I saw her number on my phone, I would ignore it, or reply with a curt text message. Sometimes I waited until I returned home to deal with her. By the time I got there, she'd be furious. Eventually we were barely communicating. After a while, she stopped complaining when I left. The ironic thing was that when I escaped to the cigar lounge or sat alone in the backyard to drink, all I would daydream about was our happy past vacations and other blissful times with my family. I had to get away from them in order to imagine a happy life.

Many men reading this may recognize themselves in my actions. If you're holding this book in your hands, you've probably reached this same moment, a time when you feel like you don't know how to be the dad your family needs. Maybe you spend time with rare scotch and a cigar, or you're off in the garage with a cigarette and a beer, or you stay later and later at work because it just seems easier than facing the family. You know how to make money to support the family, and you know you love your kids, but suddenly that's not enough.

Men want to battle a crisis, to make the plan and go after the goal with everything they have. But nothing about raising children is straightforward. No two children follow the same route, so where do you start? As I sat there night after night, I very nearly lost everything: the love of my wife, my place as the father to my children, and the chance to help my son become the good man he is destined to be.

R.J. has come so far, since that summer of scotch and cigars, when he barely spoke and wouldn't look any of us in the eye. And as a family, we've all come incredibly far. I never could have imagined the life I am living now, from the perspective of my spot at the Grand Havana. Holly and I are closer than we've ever been. And no one—including me—would have predicted then that R.J. would turn out to be a talented athlete, a fine musician, and the center of a big group of friends. Who knows where he (and we) will be ten years from now?

Nearly a decade ago, when R.J. was diagnosed, I wished there was a book that could help me navigate through those dark times, a story of hope that acknowledged the tragedy, but also could help a dad like me see the better times that were just ahead. But in the end, it was R.J.'s breakthrough moments that sustained me, changed me, and restored the bond between me and Holly. The same can be true for you and your child.

I'm not a doctor or an expert. The tips and counsel I offer are born from my experience. I hope that by sharing my story, I can help men find a way to open up about the emotions that we often don't or can't express, and women can understand more about the different way men deal with their troubles. If your family is experiencing a rough patch, my wish is that our story can be the ray of hope that helps you see your way through.

PART ONE

R.J.'s Story

1

DREAMS OF EVERY DAD

I was waiting for the baton as the anchor of the Magee Junior High track team's 4 × 400 meter relay. We were a pretty good team, but we were facing one of the best schools in Tucson. We had fallen behind in each of the three previous legs, and as I stood there anticipating my turn, I couldn't believe the distance I would have to make up in order for us to win.

I had come from behind before, but never from eighty meters back. When I got the baton and I saw how far my opponent was ahead of me, I thought, *Just run smooth. Maybe you can make up some ground and keep it respectable.*

As I rounded my first turn, my opponent had already begun the back straightaway. Then I heard my dad yell out, "GO GET 'EM, ROD!"

I felt adrenaline rush through my body, and I began to run. Not just to put on a good show, but to win!

In anything you do, most of success is the simple belief that you can win. At that moment, I believed I could, and I ran that way. I slowly closed the gap and closed the gap and closed the gap.

We came to the final turn of the race, and I had him in my sights. I could see him, but he couldn't see me. I passed him with twenty meters to go. We won the race and we went on to win the meet.

That day I learned that "it ain't over till it's over" was not just a cliché. Champions understand how to take advantage of an opportunity. They can recognize weakness, see the opening they need to win, and believe in it. That day, my dad had made me believe that I could do anything. That's the father I wanted to be to my son.

My dad had made the most of whatever gifts he had and any chances that came his way. As a child, he got up at five every single morning to do his chores. Money hadn't come easily to his family, and everyone had to pitch in. His father worked three jobs, on a neighboring farm, in construction, and as a handyman. At the break of dawn, Grandpa was in his truck going down the road picking up things to fix.

Dad was good at school and talented in sports, especially football. He got a scholarship to college, where he earned his master's in education. By the time I was born, he was a high school football coach and my mom was a schoolteacher. The University of Arizona hired him as an assistant coach when I was three.

My brother, Skip, and I were lucky to have a dad who provided us with a much easier life than the one he had had. We lived in the suburbs. Although Dad didn't have to be at work until nine, he still rose at five. He had a hard time getting my brother and me out of bed before seven A.M. Our toughest morning chores consisted of straightening our rooms and making our beds.

Even in the off-season, Dad had to work long hours. Yet with all of that on his shoulders, he took every opportunity to grab time with Skip and me. Many nights he'd come home from a long day of practice and meetings and still find the energy to go out into the street in front of our house and toss the football with us, or field a few of our fly balls or help us with our homework. Other nights we'd go to sleep not having seen him since the morning, though whenever he got home late, he'd quietly come into our rooms and sit on our beds to give us good-night kisses. I don't think I ever expressed to him how much that meant to me. He couldn't be around as much as he would have liked, but we understood how much we were in his thoughts. Despite all the demands on his time and energy, he was the opposite of a distant figure.

Once I got old enough to join team sports, I never knew when my dad would drop by practice to see how I was coming along. If he had a spare hour here or there, he would show up but stand at a respectful distance. Dad was conscious of not stepping on my coach's toes. He didn't want to make him uncomfortable, or make it seem as if he was looking over his shoulders. Although he knew twice as much as the guys who coached peewee football and baseball, he wanted me to have the experience of being coached like any other kid. He kept such a low profile that I wouldn't know he had been there until he told me when I returned home.

I liked him being there, and I wanted him to tell me what he saw in my playing and share his thoughts about how I could improve. He wouldn't offer his opinion unless we asked for it, and he never coached us until we told him that we wanted his help. He didn't want to be the dad who dragged his kid out to do extra work after practice unless his son initiated it.

I worked as hard as I could on my own, trying not to rely too much on him. When I needed to ask him for advice, I was often confused, or maybe even desperate, and ready to listen. He would always be very open about what he thought. He would show me a technique that worked better for me than the one I'd learned in practice. If my passing was a little sloppy, he might tell me to keep my elbow up to increase my accuracy. Even if he thought what the coach had told me was wrong, he would never phrase his advice in a way that would belittle the coach. He prefaced everything he said with "You've got to do what the coach says, but try this. It might help you."

Day by day, these were the ways that my dad built in us a deep reservoir of respect. The last thing we wanted to do was disappoint him. I don't ever remember him raising his voice, flying off the handle, or getting out of control. He always had a calm demeanor, but you knew when he was angry. You knew when he meant business. When he gave you that look and lowered his voice, he was serious. Most of the time he would call me Rod, but when he called me Rodney, I knew something was up.

Telling him a lie to cover up some wrongdoing would cause me more trouble than simply accepting the punishment for my mistake. He always taught us that if we told him the truth, we could work through it. He would turn the mistake into a learning experience. If I took the car and went out with my buddies even though I knew I wasn't supposed to, we'd talk about why that was wrong and what I'd realized as a result of that mistake. I'd take my punishment. *No TV. You're grounded. No game this week.*

But if I told him I hadn't taken the car and he found out (because parents always find out), he would say, "I'm going to give you one more chance to tell me the truth." It wasn't that I was afraid of him spanking me, although I did get spanked from time to time. What prevented me from getting into a lot more trouble than I did was how much I dreaded seeing that look on his face when I lied to him. When he caught me in a lie, it hurt him more than anything. And seeing that look on his face hurt me too.

The problem with me was that I was a good student, made friends quickly, and sports came easily to me. I was lucky that I could goof off all week and still know the capital of every state and ace the algebra test. But when things were going well for me, I liked to push that boundary a little bit. In that way, I seemed to be sliding through life. Every so often, I'd test to see how much I could get away with. Those were the times I forgot the powerful effect of that look on my father's face.

When I entered high school, Skip was a senior with three years of knowledge under his belt about the way the school worked.

Fortunately, he was willing to share that knowledge with me. Among the things he told me about was a storage area that separated the boys' locker room from the girls'. If you stood in a particular place, there was a way to look in on the girls when they were changing. Knowing this dramatically improved my status among the other freshman boys. I told my friends about it, but I acted as if I'd already done it so often that it didn't interest me. *You guys go right in there. Be my guests.*

Five or six of my friends went in there and made so much noise, they got caught. Although I didn't end up in the principal's office, they all told on me. Their parents called my parents, saying I set the whole thing up and made the other kids do it. My dad was furious. It took me a moment to admit I was involved. At first I was like, *What do you mean? I didn't do that.* I thought he'd be relieved that I was smart enough not to participate.

He couldn't be fooled. He knew I was the ringleader, and that disappointed him deeply. I hadn't technically lied to him, but it was as if I had. He felt as though I had dishonored our name. One of the biggest things my dad used to talk about was how he never wanted me to dishonor our name by getting involved in this kind of foolishness.

Both my brother and I were conscious of how Dad wanted us to demonstrate respect and earn everything that came our way. No special favors, and as a part of that, we anticipated and appreciated each step along the way. He marked our rites of passage and honored every milestone.

We had a basketball hoop in our backyard, and when I first

began to play, he positioned it low on the post. As I grew and be-came better at the game, he raised it a little. Each time he moved the hoop higher, he created a tougher challenge. Earn it. Work harder. Mastery is always just out of reach. As good as I got, he made me play within the rules and anticipate the next step along the path so I would want it more and appreciate it when I got there. A few of the other kids in the neighborhood were allowed to join Little League a year early. Even though I was better than kids who were two years older, I had to wait until I met the age limit. When I had a chance to move up to varsity as a freshman in high school, my dad wouldn't let me. I had to pay my dues, he said. His thinking was the same about when he would let me enter the place I most wanted to go when I was a kid: the Univer-sity of Arizona locker room after a game.

Walking into the football locker room as a five-year-old was to walk among the giants. In our town, where everything re-volved around the college, it was the greatest thing in the world to be with the players I admired. The most powerful giant among them was my dad. He wasn't as big as the players. He topped out at six feet. Yet when he spoke, everyone paid attention.

He always made his standards of behavior clear. First off, I had to wait until I was five. He said that if I were any younger, I couldn't be trusted to behave. Once I turned five, he told me that he'd only take me along if I did my chores, didn't sass back, and behaved myself in school all week.

Then the final hurdle: I had to be well mannered and re-spectful at the game. My mom, brother, and I sat in the stands on the Wildcat side, following my dad as closely as we did the game. If I acted up, Skip would go into the locker room without me.

I'd managed to keep it together for the weeks before the first home game and while the players were on the field. After the game, I was nearly jumping out of my skin as Mom led Skip and me down to the entrance where we would meet the security guard who would escort us to Dad, who was waiting at the door to the locker room. He pushed the doors open and there we were in the echoing room filled with huge men. As anxious and alert as I was, the team was relaxed, joking. Dad sat us on a big couch at the edge of the lockers, telling us not to move until he'd showered and changed.

When he finally came to get us, he led us through the locker room and introduced us to the players. He had schooled us on how to hold in our excitement, and I was aware of my father's eyes on me as I respectfully shook hands with the team. Walking out with a chinstrap or wristband from one of the guys who had scored a touchdown made me feel like I was one of the luckiest kids in the world. Even an apple or a banana from the snack table there tasted extra sweet to me.

I was allowed into the locker room at age five, but I had to wait until I was eight to join my brother on the sidelines. When we were on the field, Mom wasn't around to keep us in line and Dad was too busy to look after us. He told us exactly where to stand so that we'd be safely out of the way. The other members of the coaching staff and the security guards reinforced the order not to move from that space. Skip warned me that if I messed up, I'd never get to do it again.

Standing in that space, I heard that a lot of what Dad said to the players sounded the same as what we heard at home. "You know better than that. We went over this and over this. We practiced and practiced, and you still got it wrong. What are you thinking about? You've got to focus!" Only on the sidelines, I heard my dad raise his voice.

Watching him up close during the game when he didn't know I was looking brought my respect for him to a new level.

My dad had opened up this world to us and, at the same time, made us feel as though we belonged there. We had met his standards, followed his directions, and in doing so we received his support and affection. He had shown us how to do him proud.

With a dad like that, it's hardly a surprise that I always wanted kids. My idea of how I would be with my son was better than the opening credits of *Father Knows Best*. I would be there for him from the time he was born. I would even be there before he was born. After that, there's a bit of a gap in the highlight reel of "Dad's Greatest Plays." I could picture myself reading to my son and going for a first round of golf when he was about three or four. I imagined the long talks we would have, and in this fantasy, you can bet he was listening to me very seriously as I filled him in on everything that I knew. I was going to allow him to do all the things I hadn't done or hadn't been permitted to do. I was going to make sure that he was able to take advantage of everything.

I was trying to figure out how my dad was such a great father and take it a step or two further. That's what each generation wants to do: build on the base that their parents created and make a better life for their own children.

When Holly was pregnant and we found out that she was having twins, I was on cloud nine. I was even more excited when we learned, a few months later, after our first ultrasound examination, that we would be having a boy and a girl. "YES!" We hit the lottery. I got my boy! I prayed that everything would go well with my wife during the pregnancy and the delivery, and that my kids would be healthy.

In the weeks that followed the birth of the twins, I reached back into my childhood. My dad seemed to have figured out some of the most important things about being a dad. Yet the world my brother and I grew up in was very different from the one in which I was about to raise my children. My wife, Holly, and I were living in a nice part of Los Angeles in circumstances that were a lot more comfortable than the way either of us had lived as children. Things were so different, I did not know for certain if the ways my father raised us would apply to being a twenty-first-century dad.

I know my dad had always wished he spent more time with me and Skip. I hoped I could do more with my children because, at least for the part of the year when I was not playing football, I would have a more flexible schedule than my dad had had. And I wouldn't be playing their whole life, so when I retired, I'd have much more time to spend with them. I wanted to be that dad who took the kids to school and picked them up too. Also, I'm a different kind of man than my father in some ways. I am more passionate than him. He comes from the old school. You're not supposed to show that stuff. When he says hello, he reaches out to shake your hand and says, "Hey, how you doing?" I don't do that. I give people a bear hug.

At that moment in the hospital when I held our newborn babies, there was so much of our young lives still to be lived. I had to rush back to Philadelphia shortly after they were born, to rejoin the Philadelphia Eagles and lead the team against the Dallas Cowboys, our old nemesis. But I wasn't thinking about football. I was thinking that Holly and I were so blessed with our wonderful babies, and that there were so many opportunities before us, as we stood on the great foundation that had been laid by our loving families. Little did I realize then that R.J.'s diagnosis of autism would shake us down to that foundation, test me and our marriage, and bring me into a kind of fatherhood nothing in my life had prepared me for.

2

THE WAKE-UP CALL

The Diagnosis

Holly and I planned the twins' birth for the Monday after my team, the Eagles, faced the Arizona Cardinals. She'd had a difficult pregnancy. The doctor had ordered her confined to bed for the last three months and advised her to have a C-section. We agreed to have her labor induced so I could be there for the birth. I booked a seat on the evening's last flight to Los Angeles from Philadelphia.

As it turned out, R.J. and Ryan just didn't feel like waiting for me.

While I was on the field Sunday—in my first start in more than a year after coming off a knee injury—Holly went into labor. She called the Eagles' staff to make sure that they got me to the airport right after the game. The coach didn't tell me her contractions had started. Although there were moments when I visualized holding my twins in my arms, I was focused on the game.

Back in Los Angeles, Holly watched the game on television as her contractions became stronger and closer together. Her doctor gave her drugs to slow down her labor, and advised her to stop watching if she wanted to delay the delivery, because the game was making her more anxious. She worried that if the game didn't end quickly, I'd miss the last flight out of Philly.

Of course, the game went into overtime. My team was going crazy on the field because we'd just tied it up. Holly stared at the television in disbelief. The doctor came in and told her again that she should stop watching. He said increased stress can spoil breast milk. Holly said she'd never heard that one before. And still she couldn't stop watching.

We were lucky enough to get the ball first in overtime, and for some reason, I had a sense of urgency. I knew I had to get this game over with. I was able to get our team in position to kick the winning field goal. The minute the ball went through the uprights, the training and security staff hustled me off the field. With sirens blaring, the Philadelphia Police Department escorted me to the airport, where I luckily caught the last plane. I felt sorry for the guy who ended up next to me on the flight to LA. I hadn't had a chance to take a shower. The next day's headline in the *Philadelphia Daily News* was "OT-GYN."

In Los Angeles, the LAPD ushered me to Cedars-Sinai. A half an hour after I arrived, I held our babies in my arms.

Holly likes to describe that blissful moment when I held "the little footballs" in my hands and we, like all parents, stood in awe of what we'd done. Ryan, our daughter, was so tiny. She was only four pounds, thirteen ounces. R.J. was the dominant twin, weighing in at just over six. Both of them had jaundice. They looked like little peanuts.

Honestly, I was unprepared for the feelings they roused in me. People can tell you a million times what it is like, but unless you experience it yourself, you'll never know.

You see them and look in their eyes and know that they are a part of you. I instantly knew that I cared for them more than I cared for myself. I found out what it meant to realize that you would jump in front of a bus for someone. I would die for my kids. I love my wife, but I made a conscious decision to commit to her, to marry and love and care for her for the rest of my life. With the twins, the commitment went beyond thoughts, like a beam of light coming straight from the heart. They may have looked like yellow, wrinkly peanuts, but to Holly and me, they were the most beautiful peanuts in the world.

After forty-eight hours with them, I had to turn around and leave. That was tough, not being there for the first week. I wanted to be there to kiss them a thousand times a day. But I had to get back to Philadelphia because that Sunday we were facing the Dallas Cowboys.

The football season was hard on our young family. My team always had one day off after a game, two if we won. I would fly back to LA after the game, even if it was just for one day, then take the red-eye back to practice, exhausted. On the weeks when Holly had a break from her sitcom, she would bring the babies wherever I was. Ryan was gaining weight and catching up quickly with R.J., and both of them were so curious and alert to the world. Every week I saw such big changes in them. The weeks I couldn't see them for one reason or another, it really hurt.

By the time the football season was over, I was happy to be home so I could spend my time being the kind of dad I had always wanted to be. I wanted to be there for the fun stuff as well as for the dirty work of changing diapers. Every day with them held a surprise for me. I felt I could watch them grow and change minute by minute.

R.J. was more than hitting his milestones. He was hitting them early. He was strong and very well coordinated for a little guy. He started to walk before he hit ten months. I couldn't help but think we already had the next in a long line of Peete athletic prodigies.

R.J. was quick mentally too. I would be amazed by the way he could figure things out. As Holly and I moved around the kitchen getting their meals, he watched how we opened the childproof cabinet doors. Around the time he said his first words, at twelve months, he had figured out how to open those doors himself. I knew I was supposed to be stern with him and let him know that this was not allowed. But it was hard to fight back a smile when he looked at me with joy and pride at his latest accomplishment.

He was also into pushing buttons in the car, as many kids are. You press this button and the music turns on. Then you press this button, and the music is different. We'd let him take his toys apart and put them back together. These were just simple toys, but he'd put them back together right. When he was reassembling things, he'd look up at me like, *Heh, I got this right?* We thought R.J. was a lot like I had been as a kid: social and adventurous, with a little streak of mischief in him.

Shortly before the twins' first birthday, the whole family was invited to spend the weekend with friends of ours who have a beautiful home near Santa Barbara. We were the super-parents, with the porta-crib and everything anyone might need stuffed into the back of the car. The kids were pretty good sleepers at that point, and they slept the same schedule. We settled them down in an upstairs bedroom and fastened a childproof gate at the top of the stairs before heading down to enjoy a glass of wine before dinner with our friends. Just as we were sitting down to dinner, I heard a little shriek from R.J. Grappling hand-over-hand along the side of the archway, he came smiling into the room, ready to join the party.

Holly and I looked at each other with a mixture of very strong reactions. Oh my God! Were we bad parents for leaving him up there? How did he manage to get out of that crib, open the gate, and make his way down that long flight of slippery Spanish tile steps? What if he had cracked his head? At the same time, I was blown away by how he'd managed to make this epic journey on his own because he wanted to be where the party was. *Oh my God,* I thought, *this kid is incredible!*

Of the two of them, the child we were most concerned about was Ryan. The pediatrician had told us not to worry about her being so small, because girls catch up quickly. Unfortunately, she had muscle development problems. Her feet were splayed out, and she had trouble holding up her head well into her first year. All the family pictures from that time show big grinning R.J. looking right at the camera and Ryan with her head slumped to the side.

She was in physical therapy constantly for her first two years. She had to wear special shoes, and even when she finally started to walk, at fourteen months, she was always falling down and getting bumped and bruised. R.J. could do so many things so easily. He was a great climber and loved to crawl through things, while Ryan could be just sitting and fall over. We thought her problems were neurological, and we were always running to the doctor to get her tested.

I don't want to sound like we were frantic with worry all the time. We were happy parents who were trying to do everything right for our kids. Holly was especially good at this. She had acute mommy radar for anything that was wrong, even the tiniest sniffle or cough.

We were already planning for their futures too. We'd found out that many of our friends had enrolled their children in a very progressive school that had a great program for two-year-olds, but it was hard to get kids admitted. Holly toured the school and loved the energy and attitude of the staff as well as the smart, child-focused curriculum. We used to laugh about how silly it seemed that we were stressing out about getting our kids into preschool.

Since they had an October birthday, the twins had to wait until they were nearly three before they could start the two-year-old program. In some ways, it was good that they would start a little later than the other kids because by that point Ryan would be stronger and more coordinated.

A few months before they hit that two-year mark, Holly took the twins in for a checkup with our pediatrician. They'd had ear infections and were both coming off a course of antibiotics. Holly asked the doctor if he would delay their next round of immunizations because she thought loading them up with that much medicine while they were still a bit weak from the antibiotics might be too much for their little bodies. She believes the doctor, a very old-school, by-the-book pediatrician, brushed off her concerns as those of an overly cautious first-time mom. He said he'd immunized hundreds of children and never had any such problems.

This didn't sit right with Holly. Something about this disturbed what she calls her "mommy gut," an instinct that moms have that goes beyond what professionals say. She asked him if there was any way he could break up the measles/mumps/rubella vaccination so that they would not have to get such a potent cocktail all at once. The doctor said that that couldn't be done. Besides, the nurse said, the twins were behind in their immunizations. Part of the purpose of this visit was to get them all caught up.

Holly got even more concerned when she found out that they might be receiving more than just the MMR vaccine. She wanted to know what was in the shots and how many of them there would be. She remembers the nurse looked at her like she was psycho mommy, and told her to relax while she took R.J. in to be weighed.

Holly was sitting in another examining room holding on to Ryan, when she heard R.J. screaming, "No! Mommy!" She ran to R.J. and saw that the nurse had given him the MMR plus the second hepatitis B and the polio vaccines. The nurse said that it usually was easier with the parents out of the room.

Maybe it was easier for the nurse, but for the next eight years, nothing about R.J. would be easy for our family.

At home that night, R.J. had a terrible fever and started shaking violently, just short of something like a seizure. Holly called the pediatrician to ask him what could have caused this. Should we take R.J. to the hospital? The doctor was unruffled and told us that it was not a reaction to the shots. He recommended that we give R.J. some Tylenol to help him with the fever and he promised that R.J. would be fine. R.J. had a terrible reaction to the Tylenol and we rushed him to the emergency room late that night. We believe he went into some kind of toxic overload shock. After that, we didn't hear the words "Mommy" or "No" for about four years.

I know there is a lot of controversy in the medical community about what causes autism. Researchers and doctors reject parents' claim that vaccines, particularly the MMR, can trigger the disorder. Many parents believe that the mercury-based chemical thimerosal, which is used as a preservative in vaccines, reacts dramatically in the immature immune systems of some children and triggers autism. In the last decade, the number of vaccinations has increased dramatically; now kids get more than thirty different shots, most of them before the time they reach eighteen months.

While the government and the vaccine manufacturers have worked to reduce the amount of mercury in the vaccinations, receiving those shots gives children a big dose of toxins to process. The symptoms of mercury poisoning look an awful lot like what children with autism suffer: rocking, circling, flapping arms, walking on toes, difficulty with swallowing or chewing, digestive problems, oversensitivity to sound and touch, loss of speech or failure to speak, mild to severe hearing loss, staring and unprovoked crying, injuring self (such as head banging), social isolation, poor eye contact, and blurred vision.

The Centers for Disease Control says that the symptoms of autism start to show up around the same time that kids receive most of their shots. The CDC advises parents that this does not mean that the vaccine is the cause, and they can cite several studies to justify this position, but just to be cautious, the CDC recommended in 2001 that vaccine manufacturers reduce or eliminate thimerosal in vaccines.

Holly and I, and many of the other parents of children with autism, believe that the scientists who have concluded that there is no connection between vaccines and autism should have designed their studies differently. Our kids tend to be sensitive to foods and stimuli that other children tolerate without any trouble. We'd like to see studies performed on vaccines and children who have gluten sensitivities or are allergic to dairy, for example. We believe it might be true that kids with those difficulties shouldn't have to follow the strict vaccination schedule, at least not until their bodies have developed further.

Many of us believe that science should give this idea of a sensitivity-specific study more of a chance rather than rejecting it in favor of studies on a general population of young children. Too many families have had to suffer through a huge—and in many cases permanent—change in their children for science to turn its back on us and refuse to explore this question.

That day of the vaccination marked a major turning point for R.J. Within a week of the shots, he stopped responding to his name. Normally, when I came in to pick him up from the crib where he slept with Ryan, he'd be standing up alongside his sister. They'd look at each other and crack up, laughing at one of those private jokes that only twins can understand. Shortly after the shots, R.J. withdrew. He stopped making eye contact and he didn't laugh much. Often he'd just lie curled up in a ball staring at his hand or the wooden slats of the crib, lost in a world of his own.

Even his interest in trying to figure out how things worked changed. Before the shot, I'd watch him study the chain that went around a bicycle wheel and try to figure out how that made the wheel move. As soon as it made sense to him, he'd look my way with a big grin that said to me, *See, I figured this out!* After the shot, he was obsessive. He'd just sit there watching the chain go around and around, staring at it for hours. I'd try to get him to change activities, but he'd go right back to that chain. He also started with odd new behaviors: flapping his hands and flicking his ears. His speech stopped evolving too. He went from learning new words to saying the same thing over and over again.

We asked our pediatrician what was happening with R.J., and he acted as though what we described was no big deal. He reminded us that boys develop differently than girls. Growing up isn't a straight line, he said. He'd catch up just like Ryan had pretty much caught up with him physically.

I see now that we were willing to accept this because he was telling us what we wanted to hear. There was nothing wrong with R.J. He was just going through a phase, a temporary setback that he'd recover from before he started school in the fall. We were overjoyed when we found out that Ryan and R.J. had been accepted into our top choice for preschool. The teachers there were well trained and compassionate, and we expected that they would help R.J. learn more social skills and encourage him to make friends.

I thought that trying to keep up with the other kids would be a huge motivation for R.J. to snap out of whatever phase he was going through. Maybe once he was around the other kids he'd start to do what they did. That would help with speaking too, I thought. If R.J. really was a member of the Robinson-Peete family, there wasn't anything that could have prevented him from talking. Our pediatrician confirmed everything I had hoped about how getting R.J. out into the world would be a way to break his isolation.

The school session started in the fall, when I was right in the thick of the football season, so I wasn't monitoring R.J. as much as I would have had I been home. Holly kept telling me that R.J. didn't seem to be catching on at school, not the way Ryan was. We talked to our pediatrician again, and he told us the same thing. I repeated it back to Holly whenever she was telling me how worried she was. *He's just a little boy. He's two. Give him time. He'll catch up.*

When the football season came to a close, I took over the job of driving the kids to school. When I got them out of their car seats the first day, Ryan was ready to go. She was ready to run right into the yard where the kids had forty-five minutes to play before the indoor part of the school day began. R.J. was indifferent. I had to take him by the hand and lead him into the yard. He didn't resist. He just didn't have any enthusiasm.

After we said our good-byes, I did what my dad used to do with me. I hung back by my car and waited until I was pretty sure that the kids wouldn't be aware I was still around. I'm tall enough that I could see over the fence around the yard. I could see that Ryan had joined her friends and that they'd all run over to the finger painting table. My eyes scanned the yard to see who R.J. was playing with. He was alone by the water fountain, watching the spurts of water as he turned the knob on and off. *Look at him,* I thought. *He's always trying to figure out how things work.* As the minutes ticked by and he remained at the water fountain, my heart sank. Where were his friends? For all the money we were paying for this school, you'd think the teachers would try to get R.J. included in a group of kids or bring him over to join one of the activities. He was all alone.

The next day, when I took up my post at the fence, it was basically the same. This time R.J. was in a different corner, spinning around in circles and flicking his earlobe. Wasn't someone going to help him? Holly and I were scheduled to meet with the twins' teachers and the head of the school that next week. At that meeting, I was going to tell the teachers what I wanted them to do to help R.J. get through this tough passage.

That next week, when we arrived for our meeting at the school, I could tell something was off from the moment we entered the room and saw their grave faces. We settled into our chairs and an ominous silence settled in.

"We've talked," the head of the school said, "and we think your son is unteachable."

I looked at Holly and she looked at me. Our mouths hung open. What kid in the world is unteachable? Were they saying that R.J. didn't have the ability to learn? Who would ever say that about a three-year-old?

"We're saying there is something going on with R.J. and that we are not capable of teaching a special needs child," the head of the school continued.

All I could think was, *He's three. You don't have to teach him trigonometry.*

When we drove away from that meeting, I was angry and Holly was upset. Why are we paying all this money to this school? They didn't say, "Let's figure out how we can help this kid." They threw their hands up in the air and said, "We don't want to spend the time to do any extra work trying to teach him. This kid is not worth the effort." This was the school we'd fought to get the kids into.

By the time we got home, both of us had cooled down a bit.

We had to admit that we had concerns about R.J. and how his recent setbacks had made Ryan more clingy. The first thing we decided to do was take R.J. out of the school. Then we began our search for an expert who would check out our kids and tell us if there was anything that we needed to be concerned about.

Holly asked around and found the best pediatric specialist in Los Angeles. She was booked months in advance, and it was difficult getting an appointment for the twins to see her. Fortunately, she had a cancellation, and we grabbed it. It was excruciating to sit in that waiting room for three hours while the twins were in her office with her. We had no idea what was going on. She didn't have an observation window so we could see how they were responding to her. We were on pins and needles.

She finally called us in and we took our seats. Holly grabbed my hand.

"Your son is autistic," she said. "And your daughter is too."

Holly started to cry and the doctor handed her a box of tissues. I stared straight at this doctor in disbelief. She'd said it in such a cold way. For a specialist who had to deliver devastating diagnoses all the time, this woman had absolutely no bedside manner.

"There is a spectrum of autistic behavior, and your son is very low-functioning," she said. "Your daughter functions at a higher level. You're going to have to get your son into a program right away. He'll need speech, physical, and occupational therapy and special tutoring."

Holly was bawling by this point. I was surprised she was able to hear what the doctor was saying.

"I'm trying to prepare you as parents. I'm going to be honest with you," she said. "He's never going to be able to look you in the eye. He'll never be able to tell you he loves you unprompted. He'll never tell you he's hungry. You'll have to learn how to read his clues."

Holly's hand was gripped tight with mine while she disintegrated in the chair next to me. I couldn't believe what I was hearing. He had made eye contact. He used to let me know when he was hungry. How can she use the word "never"? This couldn't be my R.J. she was talking about. Not my boy!

"It's my experience that kids his age and at his level of severity don't generally come out of this. I want you to be prepared that this is a real uphill battle for him. If you don't start right away with these treatments, he will slip further and further into the autistic world," she concluded.

Never during the hour we spent with her did she say, *Here is our plan. Call this person for speech and this person for occupational therapy. There are a couple of schools in town that do great with kids with autism and use my name when you call. And check his diet out because there might be something going on with his digestion. Here's a nutritionist who is familiar with the kinds of digestive problems kids with autism have. You need to get him another test to see what things he is allergic to that might affect his autism.* None of that. Just the cold evaluation.

There was nothing I could do. As a man, you want to be able to protect your family. You want to be able to soothe your wife. There was nothing I could say because this so-called expert had just evaluated our kid, but she'd also robbed me of all of my power. "Robbed" is the right word. *I'm giving you this diagnosis and you've got to take it because I am the expert.*

We walked out of her private office to collect the twins. Ryan was very affectionate, but she looked a little confused as to why Mommy was crying. R.J. was oblivious. We put them back in the car, and as we were driving back home, I had an overwhelming feeling of hopelessness. I felt like a failure as a parent and I started to blame myself. I had wanted to be the kind of dad who was there for them all the time. Why didn't we recognize this earlier? Was this hereditary? Did we do something wrong during the pregnancy?

We had been responsible parents. We had asked the right questions. Where had we failed them?

We got back into the house and went through the motions of feeding the kids and getting them ready for bed. I don't remember anything of that evening. My mind was so clouded. I wanted something to do, someone to blame, but I had no target for my feelings. Holly couldn't stop crying. And in a few days, I had to leave. Football winter mini training camp was starting again. Thank God I was playing for the Raiders in Oakland, so I would be close to home.

3

DENIAL, ANGER, AND
EVERYTHING IN BETWEEN

I couldn't stop thinking about R.J. on the plane to winter mini football camp. That word "never" kept rattling around in my mind. I was so angry. He'll *never* look us in the eye. He'll *never* tell us he loves us. How could that doctor say "never" about a child who was only three years old? He had a whole lifetime ahead of him. The doctor had not offered us a single word of hope or encouragement. She scribbled down a suggestion for a school in Santa Monica called Smart Start, but told us that there was a waiting list and it would probably be two years before R.J. could begin a program. Two years! Yet she told us that his therapy needed to start right away. Where was our "Welcome to Autism" handbook? Instead it was "Welcome to *Never* Neverland."

I didn't want him to be labeled and confined by the limits that labels bring. This was something I took personally.

I grew up fighting labels and overturning predictions. When I was a young player in high school, there were only two black quarterbacks in the NFL. Both of them had had to fight hard to get those positions. Warren Moon played quarterback in Canada for five years before they'd let him play as a QB in the NFL. On the wall of my high school bedroom, I had a poster of my hero, Jim Harris, who played for the Rams, and was the first black player to start a season as a quarterback. Even though Harris and Moon had succeeded, the conventional thinking in the world of football was still that black men could not be quarterbacks.

Through high school, coaches told me I should switch positions because no college team would ever let me play quarterback. Some of the colleges that tried to recruit me said they planned to move me to wide receiver or defensive back. But I chose USC, because they'd let me play the position where I would be my best. Despite leading my USC team to the Rose Bowl twice, when it came time for the NFL Draft, nine quarterbacks were drafted before me—some of them from schools you've never heard of. I just took it as *They are wrong, and I'm going to prove them wrong*. I ended up playing as an NFL quarterback for sixteen seasons. That's where I was coming from with R.J.'s diagnosis: *It's a label, someone else's idea of who you are.*

I believed that the specialist who'd evaluated the kids was trained to look for something and she was determined to find it—even if it didn't necessarily apply.

Holly's reaction to the news also inadvertently helped me to build my denial about the truth of the situation. After she had time to think about what the doctor had told us about the twins, her mommy gut screamed that the doctor was wrong about Ryan.

Holly wrote the doctor a letter thanking her for seeing the kids, but objecting to Ryan's diagnosis. She agreed that Ryan might have some issues, but they weren't autism. The doctor reluctantly arranged to evaluate Ryan again. Sure enough, after that second visit, the doctor apologized. She said that Ryan had poor muscle tone and that she might need some occupational therapy, but she wasn't on the autistic spectrum. As far as I was concerned, if the doctor was wrong about Ryan, then there was a good chance she was wrong about R.J. too.

Our pediatrician said he'd never liked the doctor who diagnosed R.J. He didn't trust her. Hers was just one person's opinion, he said. He suggested that I find another specialist to take a look at the kids. Maybe R.J. was just having trouble focusing. Other people I talked to had mentioned the possibility of attention deficit disorder or attention deficit hyperactivity disorder.

My anger and denial left me in a lonely world. Holly didn't dispute the specialist's diagnosis of R.J.'s condition. Once she stopped crying, picked herself up, and brushed the dirt off her shoulders, Holly was fierce. She charged with all her energy in the opposite direction from me by trying to figure out what we had to do for R.J. Holly bought dozens of books on autism and books of advice on how to raise a child with special needs. Although there wasn't much on the Web about autism back in 1999, she trawled through every Web site she could find. She spoke with friends and activated a network of parents, trying to find other families who had received this diagnosis, so she could find out how they'd handled the situation.

Often, when I was home for a few days, she'd press a book she'd found helpful into my hand to try to get me to read it. But I didn't want to have anything to do with that. I still thought that when the season was over and I could spend every day with him, we would fix this our own way. I'd be his dad and I'd snap him out of this. In the meantime, I didn't want to put too much pressure on him. I believed that we all had to chill out and not get all hysterical. After all, Ryan had all those muscular problems, and she'd made huge improvements in the last year.

Yet during that training season, with all that lonely time on my hands while I was away from the family, I couldn't help but look back over the way R.J. had changed in the months since the vaccinations and reexamine how I'd explained away his behavior.

R.J. was a fussy eater, and the pediatrician had recommended that we supplement his diet with a nutritional drink that would provide him with all his vitamins. The kind he liked best came in a banana flavor. Holly and I had made up a little song to get him excited about drinking it. "Banana juice, banana juice, banana juice." After the vaccinations, once we started him singing that, he'd sing it for hours at a time. "Look at him," I'd say to Holly. "He really likes that banana formula." In trying to find fragments of the ways in which R.J. used to delight us, I was refusing to see what was right in front of my face. Yes, he was singing, but in a repetitive fashion. His voice was without music or joy.

I'd written off some of the signs of his withdrawal by telling myself that he was just doing his own thing. When I came back for one of those overnight visits during the training season, all I wanted to do was hug and kiss the kids and show them how much I loved them. But things that I'd thought were cute and funny now seemed like signals that I should have picked up on. *Oh, he's still into those cars I gave him. Look at the way he lines them up against the wall, always in the same order. He's a neat kid. That's good that he's naturally tidy. We won't have any trouble getting him to straighten up his room.*

R.J. continued to be interested in the way things worked, but as he regressed, he'd stare at the same object for hours. I got him a remote controlled car, but he didn't care about the remote or about driving the toy. Instead, R.J. would lift up the car and look underneath to see why the wheels turned, then rolled it back and forth on the ground. Back and forth, back and forth, obsessively.

When I was home for a day or two, we liked to sit together as a family and watch a movie. Although R.J. sat with us in front of the TV, now he didn't really watch the movie. He would place his face right in front of the DVD player so he could look at the controls. He made the disc come in and out, in and out. None of us could watch the movie with him popping that thing in and out, so I got him to stop. Then I noticed the way R.J. watched television.

The plot of the show and the emotions of the characters on the screen seemed to make no impression on him. If he paid attention to the program, he would fixate on a line and repeat it over and over again. While I was still in denial, I would think that was cute. *Oh, he liked that line in the Elmo song.* How could I have missed the fact that after the program was over, he would say that line all day long while he rocked back and forth? I'd explained it away by saying he was rocking to the music. *He's doing his thing.* Now Holly had given me a new word for it. She said the doctors called this behavior "stimming."

Stimming is a word from the world of autism, an abbreviation for the repetitive movements that children on the spectrum make to soothe themselves when they get overloaded by the world. Before R.J. was diagnosed, I didn't know anything about autism beyond what I'd picked up from watching *Rain Man* twenty years before. The character that Dustin Hoffman played was a savant. He knew everything about little slices of the world. He could rattle off a stream of facts almost as fast as you could download a document, but he didn't know what any of it meant. I didn't want to believe that R.J., who had been such a clown, so charming and eager to please, could end up like that character, whose only emotion was distress and who never made eye contact. R.J. would snap out of it. We just had to give him a little time.

I had never before felt so separated from what was going on in my family. When I came home from the last mini training camp before the regular season began, Holly told me that she had visited the school that the doctor who gave us the diagnosis had recommended and she had enrolled R.J. there. The teachers at Smart Start were specially trained to handle children with autism. It was hard for me to hide my disappointment when I went to see the place. I had trouble accepting that this was going to be R.J.'s daily reality.

We'd had the twins in a school where everything was state-of-the-art—beautiful grounds, spacious buildings, a cheerful staff, all very well funded by some of Hollywood's superstar parents. Smart Start was off a boulevard that was clogged with traffic. It was walled off behind huge gates masked with black material that cast long shadows over the playground. I guess the material was there to keep the kids from getting distracted by the traffic and the passersby, but even though the playground was filled with colorful toys, the smallness of the yard and the height of its walls made it seem cramped and restrictive.

Parents were allowed to stay for the first forty-five minutes of the school day, but being there made me uncomfortable. The teachers were kind, attentive, and well trained, but the other students alarmed me. The school took kids from all points on the spectrum, and some of them were very low-functioning and uncommunicative. The first time I visited, one of R.J.'s classmates was making a dull noise and banging his head on the wall. As I hung back and watched the class, another child had a seizure, which is common among kids on the spectrum. R.J. was quiet and withdrawn. The place seemed like an asylum to me, and I wondered if R.J. felt that way too.

When I got home at the end of the season, the family I returned to was run by Mama's Rules. Holly had put many programs into place without consulting me. When he'd completed his four-hour school day, R.J. had occupational therapy, speech therapy, and some other treatments, depending on the day. He was coming home at six or seven o'clock at night and Holly was planning to add to it. This was an everyday deal, and I felt this was way too much for a kid to handle. I was fighting this. I told her, "We've got to pull back a little." She said, "No. We've only got a small window of time in which we can make an impact on him. If he gets to seven or eight and we haven't gotten him talking on his own and expressing himself, he'll be lost to us forever. We've got to do it all."

Of course, I know now that what I should have done was praise Holly for how hard she was working on trying to help R.J., but at the time I wasn't feeling it. I didn't want him to be in the world she was creating for him. I think all parents want to give their kids a life that is better than the one they had. The way Holly was arranging his time, R.J. wasn't going to have any childhood. No play, no fun, nothing but this crazy school and therapy forty hours a week. "Why does it have to be like that?" I objected. "We're going to burn this kid out."

When I got him alone, I would grab him and look him in the eye. I believed that this was a little boy who really needed his father. Those teachers at his first school had ignored him, and his mom was trying to find programs and therapists that would help him along. All of that was fine, but I believed that if he and I had more one-on-one time, then I'd be able to coax out the boy he used to be.

Just having his dad around could make a big difference. And to overcome some challenges, you've got to be around people who will motivate you. That's the first step in motivating yourself. You've got to think about the best times in your life and believe that those can happen again. That's the kind of thinking that can get you out of your rut. Those were the tools that I was taught by my dad. And that was how I wanted to teach my son.

I decided that I would work with him. He's an extension of me, and if anyone could help him, it had to be me. *Despite what everyone else says, I'm going to spend day and night doing anything I can to get him out of that world, because I'm the dad with the magic touch. I don't care what the doctor says. I may not have a PhD, but he's my son and we are going to fight this together.*

Physically, he was fine. He could do everything that the other kids could do and, in some cases, even a little more. I thought that by playing sports with him, I could figure out how to bring him out of his strange world. I took him to a nearby park so that we could play catch or soccer, or any other game he wanted to try. The back of our SUV looked like the inside of a sporting goods store. I had every different kind of ball and bat and mitt, hoping that one of them would catch his attention. If we were lucky, we could get some of the other kids in the park to join in too.

He was always happy to go with me, but most of the time he didn't want to interact once we got into the park. He might find a rock down by the creek and throw it in the water. Then he'd find another and throw that in too. I'd get a bat from the car and put his hands around it, but he just wasn't interested. He'd look at me with glazed eyes, as if he couldn't get what I was telling him. Then he'd drop the bat and go back to the creek.

But not every day was like that. Sometimes I'd get him to engage with me. For example, one day I kicked him the soccer ball and he kicked it back. I left the park that day thinking that I'd made big progress with him. Then days would go by when I couldn't get him to pay attention to the soccer ball again. That one afternoon with the soccer ball wasn't a milestone; it was just that day's obsession—forgotten as soon as we stopped.

After our sessions in the park, I always took R.J. to McDonald's. Sometimes it was easy. He'd tell me what he wanted, and if the place was quiet, we'd sit together and have our snack. But more often than not, it took me five minutes to get him to look at me and tell me what he wanted. If the place was crowded, he'd get agitated and start to scream and I'd have to get him out of there. I always tried not to show him how upset I was. I'm sure my frustration came out at times, but I did my best.

Despite my lack of success with R.J., I still didn't want to believe that Holly had it right either. She continued to search for exactly the right kind of behavioral therapist and speech therapist—firing people and hiring people and continuing to add new things to R.J.'s already demanding schedule. I was still dragging my feet.

Like most men, I need to see the breakthroughs. I was interested in seeing results. I wasn't about the small wins. I wanted to see something dramatic. I saw all this money flying out the door for these different therapies that I'd never heard of before, and none of it seemed to be helping R.J. I let Holly try these things, but I still believed that if I devoted more time to R.J., everyone would see him take big steps forward.

I realize now that my determination was a cover for how

much I was really hurting. All my feelings about what had happened to R.J. were in my way, so I tried to push them aside and focus on the goal of getting my boy back. I believed that I needed a laserlike focus on that main objective. Although that laser focus gave me blinders to what else was happening around me, and it restricted me from seeing how much of a gulf was opening between me and Holly.

After those difficult days at the park with R.J., I'd come home and Holly and I would go through our normal evening routine, ignoring the wall that was steadily building between us. I think each of us was holding a grudge against the other. We were working as hard as we could in our own different ways to help R.J., but we'd stopped listening to each other. I sometimes got frustrated with R.J., but I would never share that feeling with Holly, because to do so might open the door to her criticizing my approach with him. We were not a team. We each had our secrets and our secret resentments.

Routine covers up many things. Both of us went through the motions of caring for our children, and there was tenderness in the room—but none of it was between us. There were now so many things that we couldn't talk about unless we wanted to have a knock-down, drag-out fight. This was a terrible thing for two parents, two lovers, who thought of ourselves as each other's best friend. All the love we had for each other had been redirected toward the kids. That emptiness between me and Holly was another aspect of my loneliness, and it was something that I was almost too frightened to bring up, because I didn't know where that conversation would lead. It had led so many times before to an argument that it was just easier to say nothing.

After R.J. had been at Smart Start for a while, we were asked to attend a review session in order to assess his progress. All his teachers were going to be there, along with his speech, occupational, and behavioral therapists.

The focus of his behavioral therapy was something they call floortime, which is when the therapist gets down on the floor and plays with the child, letting the child decide what he wants to do and then talking to him about it. The idea is to engage the child in something that he likes and demonstrate to him that you're also interested in what he's interested in, bringing him into a comfortable situation where he can express himself. You meet on his terms, but you have the chance to subtly nudge him along.

R.J.'s floortime therapist had taught us her techniques, but it was another one of those strategies that seemed a bit overhyped to me. She was trying to teach me to play with my son! I already knew how to play with him. I'd been doing that for his whole life. At the review session, they asked me to get down on the floor and interact with R.J. I was eager for a chance to show them that I already knew how to do this. And I was going to do it my own way.

R.J. had a fire truck and he was running it back and forth on the floor. I got down next to him and asked him how he was doing. He didn't respond. I asked him what he was playing with. He didn't answer. Was he having fun? I asked. Still no response.

In my memory, this went on for ten painful minutes, but Holly recalls it being a lot shorter than that. I believed I was the dad with the special touch who was going to show them how it was done, but it was a total disaster. He didn't interact with me at all.

His floortime therapist asked if I'd mind if she gave it a try. She started asking R.J. specific questions like "What do the wheels do?" and "Why does the fire truck have a ladder?" R.J. said they used the ladder to save people. She asked R.J. when the firefighters needed to save people. R.J. told her that they would get people when their building was on fire.

Holly was looking at me smugly. We'd all just seen the proof that I didn't know what I was talking about. I was burning up, frustrated and angry. I couldn't wait to get out of that meeting.

We got in the car and Holly wanted to talk about it.

"You don't get it, do you?" Holly asked me. "Can't you see what happened today? You do not know what you're doing. Admit it then."

"I don't want to talk about it," I said.

"This is a twenty-four/seven, three hundred and sixty-five fight," she said. "Unless you are trained and know the right techniques to identify what triggers what in a child, you are going to be spinning your wheels and we haven't got that much time."

Obviously, what I didn't get at the time was that we were dealing with a bigger force than I could grasp. R.J.'s problems were neurological and had a physical component. They were not controllable by will alone. They could not be addressed by defiance or discipline, which were the great dad tools I had learned from my own father. This wasn't something that I wanted to admit to Holly or even to myself.

I dropped Holly and R.J. off at home and told Holly I had something I needed to do. I drove straight to the Grand Havana Room, got a Montecristo #2 and a Macallan eighteen-year-old scotch and sat in my favorite chair.

Holly had set me up, I was sure of it. She'd conspired with those teachers to embarrass me. They had all looked at me as if I had not served my son well. She was just trying to prove her point, and she was in cahoots with all those people at Smart Start. Those people didn't know what they were talking about. I hated that school and I hated all those people over there. I even hated dropping R.J. off there.

When someone tells you something—as Holly had been telling me for months—you can either hear it or not. But when someone shows you with your own eyes that you're wrong, it's a serious blow. I was denying what had happened at R.J.'s school, but deep down inside I knew that I was wrong and that Holly was right. I was failing my son because of my ego.

That's what Holly had been trying to tell me all these months. She'd never said I was a failure. She encouraged me to get involved. She wanted to engage my heart and show me how much R.J. needed me. But men tend to put things in the starkest terms. This was a boy—my son!—who needed me. I had failed him. And I was angry at her for making me realize it.

When I came home, the kids were in bed.

"We have to talk about this," she said. "I think today you

finally saw what I've been trying to show you. You saw it, you felt it, and you have to deal with it."

"They are not the experts on everything," I said.

"They are the experts on this," she explained.

"You set me up. That's what was going on there today," I said. "What happened there was something you arranged in advance."

"You think I'd do something like that? You think I've got time to stage stunts? Is that what you really think?" she said. "Look, I don't know how much clearer it has to be for you. Either you're on board on this, or you've got to go."

I looked at her in disbelief.

"We live in a totally different reality now," she said. "You've got to put aside everything you know and all the things you thought about what kind of a life we were going to lead. We've got to be in this together. We've got to have a team around us now. It's Team R.J. Everybody in his life has to be on board."

"I am on board," I said. "I'm trying to help my son. I don't agree with some of the things you've been doing and the way you're rushing him around keeping him tied up in therapies all day long. He's my son, and I want him to have a childhood like I had."

"Listen, it's not about you," she said. "It's about him. Seriously, this is hard enough. I can't do it without you, but I can't do it with you like this. You have to get on board. I know this is not what you envisioned it being like when you thought about having a son. You thought you'd have him in the locker room like your dad had you in there. You imagined all these things that your son could be. But this is your damn son and you're going to have to deal with this at some point and if you don't, you're going to have to go. I can be sad and wallow in this all by myself. I don't need you dragging me down. And I am not bluffing."

Suddenly I started to cry. I felt so helpless. I didn't want to lose my family. And I never, ever wanted to harm my son. Holly was right. I had to put my ego aside.

All this time I had been thinking that the right way to be a dad—the way my father had raised me—was to show your son that you set standards for him that you expected him to meet. Like my dad had been for me, I sought to be a model to R.J. for how a man should behave. Gradually, with the combination of a gentle guidance, affection, and a firm hand, he would earn the right to be part of a man's world, and I would be the one who had opened that world to him. Every one of those ideas had just shattered along with my state of denial. If I was going to do what had to be done to save my son, I couldn't expect him to join me in my world. Holly was right. The only way this could work for R.J. is if I got down on the floor and joined him in his.

"Where do I start, Holly?" I asked her. "What do you need me to do? I'll do whatever it takes for R.J."

4

TEAM R.J.

When I moved past my denial of R.J.'s condition, I was surprised by how I felt. I felt liberated. Sure, at first I'd mourned the vision I'd had of the kind of father I would be to R.J. And I understood that I had to let go of all the images of fatherhood that I'd received from movies and television—everyone from Ward Cleaver to Cliff Huxtable. I wanted to have as loving a relationship with R.J. as I'd enjoyed with my own dad, but I had come to terms with the fact that it couldn't be exactly the same. I couldn't simply cut and paste my dad's style of being a father onto me and my son.

My dad used to let me know I was in trouble by sternly calling me "Rodney" instead of his usual "Rod." That was useless to me and R.J. because R.J. had trouble responding to his name at all, let alone picking up the difference between my calling him R.J. and Rodney Jackson. It typically took us two or three tries to get him to look up from what he was doing. Often, I had to move over to where he was and stick my face right in front of his to get his attention. He focused intensely on whatever was right in front of him because the rest of the world was too much for him to handle.

My dad's technique of delaying a reward, making me wait until I was five to go into the locker room, wouldn't work either. R.J. couldn't plan that far ahead. And for R.J., the locker room wasn't a reward. I'd tried to take him there, but he'd found the noise and the strangers overwhelming. While other players' kids did as I had, moving among the team and getting a chinstrap or a wristband from one of their heroes, R.J. felt most comfortable sitting inside my locker where he could shut out the chaos. I hadn't liked the way he was behaving, but I thought at the time that it was just a phase. Maybe Dad was right. Four was too young to be in the locker room. But when my denial broke, I realized that this ritual that I had valued so much when I was his age wasn't something that he enjoyed. I had to accept that it was something that he might never enjoy.

Who was he? This little guy I'd lived with almost every day of his life was a mystery to me. I didn't understand him.

I thought back to an afternoon before we'd received the diagnosis, when R.J. disappeared and scared Holly and me to tears. We blamed him for being disobedient, but what was that episode really about? That day two years earlier, I was in one part of the house and Holly was in another. Each of us thought that the other one was watching R.J. When we saw each other in the kitchen, we realized that he'd been out of our sight for at least five minutes.

As we searched the house yelling his name, that five minutes became ten, then fifteen. We couldn't imagine that he'd walked out the front door, so we ransacked the closets and the little secret places in the house that only children could fit into. No R.J. Our panic level rose.

We lived in a gated community so we were sure that if he'd managed to slip out the door, then at least he wouldn't have gotten out onto the busy street that ran alongside our neighborhood. We jumped in the car and drove through the streets around our house for nearly an hour yelling his name out the window. Our minds were filled with horrible ideas of what could have happened to him.

Finally we decided that we had to look outside the gate. Although it seemed inconceivable to us, he might have slipped past the guardhouse unnoticed. Thinking of him toddling into the four lanes of traffic on Coldwater Canyon or hiding in the twists of Mullholland Drive was too much to bear. We decided that we needed to cover more ground more quickly, so we headed home so that Holly could get her car and we could search separately. When we pulled into the driveway, we gasped. There was R.J. sitting cross-legged on the roof.

The house had two sections, with one part a single story in height, and the other rising to two stories. There was a window on the second floor that opened to the eaves of the roof of the shorter piece of the house. R.J. must have found that window open and crawled out. He sat at the edge of the roof, stimming, flapping his hands at his ears, lost in his dream world.

Holly burst into tears. She'd been crying from time to time during our frantic search, but seeing him there so close to the edge of the roof sent her over an edge of her own. I realized that I had to handle this carefully. I didn't want to startle him. I needed to get to him before he moved even an inch. As Holly stood in the driveway talking to him through her tears, I went into the house, up the stairs and wedged myself partway out the window to coax him back to safety.

When I got him back, I kneeled down and placed my hands on his shoulders so I could look him right in the eye as I explained how much danger he'd been in. "This is a dangerous situation, R.J., do you understand me?" I said. He didn't react to the tone of my voice. "Sitting on the roof is not something you can do. Did you see how far you would fall if you took a wrong step? You do not just crawl out the window. Everything you do, you have to ask Mommy or Daddy first."

For all the emotion I had packed into my voice, R.J.'s face didn't indicate that he was picking up on my urgency or my concern. When you speak that strongly to a small child, he might not understand exactly what you're saying, but the intensity of your expression usually makes him cry or react in some way. R.J. seemed oblivious. At the age of three, it didn't seem possible that he could be calculating enough to ignore me on purpose. What would it take to get him to realize what danger was?

What motivated him? What could I hold out to him as a reward that would get him to obey his mother and me? That year, we were fortunate enough to get excellent seats for the

Nickelodeon Kids' Choice Awards, a place where the twins would get to see SpongeBob SquarePants and all their other cartoon heroes. We built up the event by talking to them about it for weeks before we went. When one of them wasn't doing what we wanted, we'd warn that if they didn't behave, they wouldn't get to go to the show. Ryan was focused on the big day and very excited when it arrived. But when we entered the hall, R.J. started screaming and his arms flailed around. We tried to get him to look at SpongeBob and some of his other favorites, but no matter how I held him or what I said, he just screamed louder. Quickly, Holly and I decided it would be better for everyone if we just went home.

Those were the extremes: R.J. on the edge, both literally and figuratively. But most days he didn't inhabit those extremes. He was a quiet guy with his own set of interests that I'd only begun to explore.

For a while, I hadn't seen him as a unique individual with his own personality because I was so busy trying to see him as a reflection of me. I had a picture of him that I treasured, a portrait that we'd taken when he was one. I'd placed a little football in his hands, Daddy's little man: the agile guy who had walked at ten months and braved the stairs in a stranger's house to join the party, my Mini-Me.

In a way, it seemed like an abandonment of R.J. to mentally remove that little football from his hands. Yet I knew I would be building a legacy of frustration and conflict if I spent my energy trying to turn him into something he was not. I needed to let him be himself. That's what it takes to be a great dad to the child you brought into this world: being the person who helps a child grow into the fullness of who he is. My father's style of being a dad was tailored to nurture and control two boys who were active, curious, and had a tendency to get into a little bit of trouble. R.J. presented a completely different set of challenges. He needed me to be a different kind of dad. The problem for me was I didn't know exactly what kind of dad that would be.

For the first five years I played in the NFL, I had a coach who told me that to succeed, I had to get out of my comfort zone. That was a big deal for me, because I was the kind of person who liked to have a plan of action. But what the coach was telling me was to trust my instincts, my moves, and my reactions, and not be stuck in the way that I'd been coached to behave—those skills and responses that had been drilled into me by hours of practice. The idea is that at a certain point, you can only grow by moving beyond what you have been taught by those who came before you.

There always comes a time, as a player, a father, and a man, when you must stand on your own. Of course, you must acknowledge and respect everything you have learned. But that moment when you recognize that you're standing on your own, you've got to trust that you're going to do the right things un-coached. You've got to trust that you know what to do, even if you don't know exactly what that next move should be.

That's why getting past the denial about R.J. had opened up other possibilities in my life. It changed me. Everything that I had learned to do a certain way didn't apply to this situation.

There was a different reality out there. Not only with my son, but in other aspects of my life. I had to change, and I wasn't sure exactly how. Though I'd been a dad for four years, it was as if I was just beginning.

I had to start by seeing my son for exactly who he was.

Not my boy, I'd been saying. I didn't want to accept their labels. He's not this. He's not that. In starting to be a father to my actual son, I had to see him without trying to deny or explain. How could I reach that boy on the roof?

The day after that turning point conversation with Holly, when I took R.J. to Smart Start, the whole place seemed different to me. Now I realized why they say that kids who have autism are on a spectrum. There are huge differences among them. I'd noticed that before, but mainly only to justify in my mind my belief that R.J. didn't belong there.

There were some kids who were completely off in a dreamworld, rocking back and forth. R.J. had those moments. Others were agitated and would twirl around flapping their arms. My son had his own version of that too. When the teachers tried to get the most severely affected students to pay attention to what was going on in class, some of those children would lash out. They would scream and flail. While it was sometimes difficult to get R.J. engaged in what was going on, he didn't have many meltdowns. He was quiet and kind to everyone. So while I recognized some version of these behaviors in R.J., I wasn't sure which of these signs of his condition indicated his major problems, or where I should begin to help him.

Children with autism are so different from one another that doctors sometimes call autism an "umbrella diagnosis," because there is a wide range of behaviors that fit under that umbrella. If a child exhibits several of them, a poorly trained doctor might say that the child has autism, even if the child might have a different problem, such as sensory processing disorder. Sharon Lowery, the director of Smart Start, calls it a "wastebasket diagnosis." Just throw everything in there until you have enough to get a diagnosis.

Sharon is an angel. She is kind, compassionate, and tireless. And she's an expert at handling parents when they come through her door with their nerves rubbed raw by the double whammy of their child's diagnosis and the dashing of their dreams. She wanted to do the same thing I wanted to do: to throw out the label, look at the different aspects of R.J.'s diagnosis, and see him for who he was and what he needed.

One of the first things I learned was to toss away the "nevers," because we don't know if any of that is true. If you keep thinking about the "nevers," it's hard to conceive of the "possibles." Once Sharon and her staff had a good look at how autism affected the way R.J. took in the world, she created a plan to attack his deficits, and we all got to work making it happen. In work, there's hope—this was the opposite of what we'd found with the first doctor. That's the first job of anyone who helps you and your kid face challenges: to re-set the starting blocks for hope.

R.J. had lost a lot of language when autism shut him down.

He still said some words, but they didn't make any sense. He was remote, as if he had a curtain around him. He also didn't express his needs spontaneously, even pressing ones like hunger or thirst. His teachers said that he had what they called motor planning issues. If the next activity was to get his lunch box from his cubby and sit at the table to eat, he seemed to grasp what he was supposed to do, but he had a hard time figuring out how to go about it. There was a breakdown between having an idea and getting his body to act on it. Ryan would have just jumped up and run over, without a thought. R.J. stood frozen, unable to decide which foot to move first or what direction to go in. That was why he sometimes seemed stuck and passive. Moment by moment, the teachers had to prompt him every step along the way.

After our daily forty-five-minute time for class observation was over, I'd linger at the window to watch how R.J. fit in. In my own way, I was plotting where he was on the spectrum. On the plus side, I could see that he was an incredibly intuitive little guy. He scanned the classroom, always watching, always trying to figure things out. Maybe I'm projecting my own feelings here, but I thought I saw him thinking, *Get me out of here. I don't belong here.* The way he appeared to evaluate his classmates contradicted the idea that kids on the spectrum do not have any intuition. Also, even though he had trouble holding a pencil or crayon and getting his body in the correct position to do work at a desk—the fine motor problems that a lot of little guys on the spectrum have—he was physically strong and well coordinated. These areas of strength were also places to focus on to start trying to bring R.J. back.

Once I fully committed to Team R.J., Holly encouraged me to take him to his appointments in order to get to know his therapists. The schedule was demanding. After the three hours a day at Smart Start, he had speech therapy. He also had physical therapy that was designed to help him tolerate the different physical stimuli the world threw at him. On top of that, he had occupational therapy for the fine motor skill deficits. There was also listening therapy at a special lab on the east side of Los Angeles, in Pasadena. This all meant hours in the car, and a lot of work for R.J.

Instead of separating myself and playing with my BlackBerry, or talking on my cell phone, as I had the times I'd taken him before, I began to pay attention to how R.J. was doing in these sessions. When he ran into trouble, I could see him trying to fight himself out of it. Something was holding him back. I could see frustration in his eyes, and the way they would get glossy when he couldn't do certain things or couldn't figure out where he was or what was going on. And I learned that if you are not really engaged in your child's sessions—if, like me while I was in denial, you're there, there but not *really* there—you just won't understand what's involved in the treatments. Seeing his therapists in action, I saw how wrong I had been to think that I could help him with no training.

In occupational therapy, he struggled with some of the simplest tasks. Many of them were things that he had done so easily before. The therapist would show him how to hold a block in a certain way, but he had the toughest time getting it to sit right in his hand. I'd see him pick up the block and then look off into the distance, not understanding why he was holding it. I was five feet away, but my heart and soul were right there next to him, trying to help him put the right block in the right hole. When the therapist asked him to do something, she carefully conveyed the request through her facial expressions, along with verbal cues in order to orient him to language. She touched him gently to suggest where his hand should be and how he could maneuver his whole arm to fit the block in the hole.

Then they worked on holding a pencil. She would say a letter and he was supposed to write it down. He'd pick up the pencil and be at a loss as to what the next thing was he was expected to do. She'd say, "Rodney, Rodney, come on." Then he'd go under the table. When he was in speech therapy, it was the same thing. The therapist would try to get him to say certain words, but he wouldn't look at the page or he'd just repeat what she'd just said.

I was frustrated because his mind couldn't click. God, why can't he get it? He just did it yesterday. It's the next day and he can't do it. Why can't I reach him? I just wanted to go over there, sit down next to him, and say, "Hey, son, let me show you how this is done. Then you can do it again. Let me help you." It broke my heart.

Dads want to see their children build from one strength to the next, getting stronger all the time. You learn this skill and then the next day you get a little bit better at it. That's the usual paradigm. This is how we succeed. But R.J. might have a great day and then he'd go back to the way he was two days before. He'd read a word, or he'd look at a letter and identify that this was A and this was B and this was C and then we'd go through all our numbers. He was on it. He'd look me in the eye when I said, "Look me in the eye." I'd tell him to repeat this sentence and he'd repeat it. One day he looked me right in the eye and said I love you. He did it! Let's go show Mom! The next day, nothing.

His therapists maintained that he was making progress, and that we could not let up. Although it was hard for us to see it, it was clear that he was working really hard. The problem kids with autism have is in understanding which of the sights, sounds, smells, and sensations are important to what they are supposed to be doing at that moment. A kid with attention deficit disorder is overwhelmed too, but he can figure out what those around him expect. For R.J., the sound of a plane flying high overhead and the sound of my voice seemed equal. How was he supposed to know which one he should be listening to? As parents, your job is to teach your child moral values. In our work with R.J., we had to teach him sensory values too. Listen to the sound of my voice. The person in front of you, the one looking at you, is more important than the jackhammer tearing up the sidewalk.

We had to keep on him when he was home—minute by minute, interaction by interaction, without a break. He needed constant stimulation. One of the big techniques was floortime, the technique I'd failed at while all the Smart Start teachers were watching. The therapists who came to our house to work with R.J. had to teach me how to interact with him in a way that would help him progress. A dad's natural mode is to tell the child what he is going to do and make sure he does it. "Sit down in this chair, boy. We're going to talk. Look me in the eye when I'm talking to you." Floortime breaks that up. They trained me to join R.J. right where he was.

Often R.J. had no idea what I was saying, so when he saw a certain look on my face, he might think that I was mad at him when I wasn't. When therapists tell you that you need to be more expressive, this doesn't mean that they want you to get louder. It means that they want you to give your child an additional clue or two about what you mean when you talk to him. The goal was for R.J. to figure out that life is constant interaction.

Let's say he pulled out a Thomas the Tank Engine puzzle. The therapists taught me to start narrating what we were doing, asking him questions every step along the way. "Okay, you've taken out a Thomas the Tank Engine puzzle. That's great! You really like Thomas. I do too. Let's do this puzzle together. Oh, that's Thomas. And oh, who is that? That's Henry! Right, R.J. We have to put the puzzle together. And who is that? Bertie? What piece goes here? Does that piece go there? Hey, it fit in the first time! Good job, R.J.!"

I had to make the most of whatever he showed interest in. Say he grabbed my keys. If I didn't mention it to him, he could end up jumbling the keys in his hand all day long. I'd say, "What are those? Those are keys. How many keys are on that ring, Rodney?

How many silver keys are there? Count them. How many round keys are there?"

Besides floortime, we used another therapy called ABA, applied behavioral analysis. This therapy was less spontaneous and more focused on a specific goal. While the two styles were at war—with the ABA therapists saying floortime was useless and the floortime therapists claiming that ABA produced little robots—Holly saw advantages in both. She was thinking outside the box, as she usually does. ABA rewards the child for desired behaviors, such as saying please and thank you, whereas floortime encourages spontaneity. We wanted R.J. to be both: a child who could be polite or spontaneous, depending on the situation.

When we'd give R.J. something, every time we had to ask him, "What are you supposed to say? What are you supposed to say? What are you supposed to say? Thank you, right?"

After a time, he'd respond, "Thank you."

"No, look me in the eye and say it."

We had to be on him all the time. We had to keep him moving and keep his mind moving. We always had to be aware of where R.J. was and what he was doing. Every minute that he slipped into his corner was a moment that was lost. If someone was cooking dinner, he or she had to stop and check to see what R.J. was doing. We needed to make sure he wasn't rocking in the corner for thirty minutes. One day he does it for thirty minutes, then he'll do it for forty-five, then for an hour, and the next thing you know, he's gone. We had to attend to it like it was an emergency, but at the same time make it seem like play.

You hear stories of people who slip into a coma and their families visit the hospital every day for years to talk to them in the hope that they'll move a finger or flicker an eye or say a word. I used to wonder if I could do that, but that was before R.J. When you are faced with something like that happening to a loved one, you do what you have to do. This journey we took with R.J. required me not just to break my denial, but to have patience and sensitivity at every moment, in every interaction with him. This was a quest to discover the heart of who he was and where he was at every moment. And a personal quest for me to discover the patience to realize that even the tiniest bit of progress counts.

Kids teach all parents to slow down and be more patient. R.J. required patience beyond anything I could have imagined, because we were never sure if what we were doing was helping him or how long it would take to see progress. They might tell us that if we did a certain exercise for a year, then he was going to improve, so in our minds we think, *Okay, it's just a year.* You can tick off the days. After a month, you are eight percent closer to that goal. But in this case, there's no certainty that it'll work. There's hope of an outcome, but there is no guarantee. But you still have to be consistent—you might still be doing this four years from now. You can't measure it with a measuring stick or plot it on a chart. It may come in leaps and bounds, and it might come in a week, but it also might not come in a year.

I say this so easily now because it has become part of what I accept in loving R.J., but I confess that this lesson didn't come easy. Before I started working along with the therapists, I would get frustrated when R.J. didn't want to do the activities I wanted him to do. I'd sit there when we took our outings to the park and watch him throw rocks into the creek and maybe ask him a couple of questions. But there was no real interaction with him.

Over the course of a year, whenever I was in town, I closely watched how the therapists worked with him. I saw that he thrived within a very structured environment. He liked to know the schedule. He needed it to help him be prepared for every activity before it started. Once I realized how much he liked to anticipate the day's schedule, I started walking him through the day when we drove to school in the morning. Who are you going to see there, R.J.? Trisha and Gary. We'd talk about what would happen first, and when they would go into the yard to play, then when they would have snack. I could look in the backseat and see a smile on his face. Knowing how the day would unfold comforted him.

Suddenly it dawned on me that I could do the same thing with him before we went to the park.

As we drove to the park, I started asking him about it so he could picture it.

"R.J., we're going to the park. What's your favorite part of the park?

"The creek."

"What do you like to do at the park?"

"I like the jungle gym."

"I like the park too, but I like to do different things there. What do I like to do?"

"Play with the balls."

"Will you help me with that? Will you help me kick the soccer ball?"

I didn't get an answer to that question. Then I thought if what he liked was knowing in advance what was going to happen, he needed to have more than just a list of activities, he needed to know what the limits were to each activity. If what he wanted to do was throw rocks in the creek, it might seem like it was taking forever to get to that if he didn't know how many times I wanted him to kick the soccer ball.

"R.J., will you help me kick the soccer ball ten times?"

"Yes."

"I need to practice throwing the football ten times. Will you help me, R.J.? Will you catch it ten times for me?"

He said he would.

"Ten times," I repeated as we got close to the park. "Ten kicks with the soccer ball."

"Ten kicks," he repeated.

"No more than twenty, right, R.J.? We are going to throw the football and you have to catch it ten times. Then we are going to the creek and we are going to throw the rock ten times. Ten, ten, and ten."

When we got to the field, I carried the soccer ball and R.J. held the football. When we got to the center, R.J. obediently placed the football on the ground and waited. He was completely focused as I kicked the soccer ball his way. He kicked it right back and we both yelled, "One!"

It was as if just shouting out that number was in itself a victory. I shot the ball back his way and we both yelled, "Two!"

The ball rumbled back over the turf, right to my instep and pow, "Three!" I was smiling as if I'd just scored a touchdown at the Super Bowl.

Such a simple thing, this back-and-forth between a dad and his son, and it wouldn't have been possible a year before.

"Four!" we yelled. There was a beautiful, big smile on R.J.'s face. We were having fun!

"Five!" He wasn't passive or closed off. He wasn't shut down. This was completely spontaneous.

"Six!" I thought this was the guy with the motor planning problem. He wasn't having any trouble planning how to respond to this soccer ball.

"Seven!" *R.J., you dog.* That last kick caused me a little trouble.

"Eight!" You know who I wished was watching my boy right then? Those teachers who said R.J. was unteachable.

"Nine!" And that doctor. I'd like to show her too.

"Ten!"

"Good job, R.J.," I said. "Ten kicks. Good job."

He didn't seem to get how much of a miracle this was to me.

"The football," he said. "Then the creek."

I'm not describing this scene to show you that at last I became the dad with the magic touch. After all the therapy we as a family had been through with R.J. in the year after he was diagnosed, I knew that my touch was far from magical. Those sessions, the hours upon hours in the car, and the endless repetition of those simple tasks had led us to this moment. R.J. presented us with his achievements, but we had to be alert and focused on him in order to recognize them. Then one day he'd do something like he did in the park. That's a milestone. That's growth. Small wins were unbelievable. That afternoon, something clicked for him. And when the results came, they sometimes came in bunches.

For weeks in his class at Smart Start, the teachers had been preparing the kids for the presentation each would need to make to the class. If you'd seen these kids, you'd know that this was a big event for them. These are children who had a hard time talking to their parents, and most of them had an even more difficult time interacting with their peers. Expecting them to stand up in front of the class and describe something in a way that all of us could understand was to ask for a considerable achievement. The teachers wanted us to help the kids at home. The first step in helping R.J. was to pick out something that he really liked and had played with so often that he would be comfortable talking about it. Strength to strength, I thought. Let R.J. capitalize on something he already knew well and build from there.

Holly and I thought about this, and decided to steer him toward something that always brought a smile to R.J.'s face—his grandfather's books. Holly's dad, Matt, played Gordon on *Sesame Street* when the show first started in the late 1960s. He also wrote a series of children's books. R.J. loved the funny characters his grandfather created and the book's simple stories about the environment.

An advantage to having him present these books was that

he'd probably paged through them a hundred times. He was very familiar with them, which meant that we wouldn't need to start from scratch. He recognized the drawing of his grandpa on the cover. He knew about *Sesame Street,* and we'd read the text of the book to him more times than we could count.

The day of the presentations, all the parents had hopeful faces. I guess we were all anticipating the worst, so we smiled as broadly as we could with our *everyone is a winner today* view of what was about to happen. One after the other, the teacher coaxed the kids out of their seats and showed them where to stand in front of the class. One little guy stood there as he was told and that was it. He wasn't able to speak. He pointed to a few things in a photo album and shook his head when the teacher identified the members of his family. Another boy was in constant movement; it was impossible to get him to stand still long enough so that you could understand what he had to say. Then it was R.J.'s turn.

R.J. got off the floor quickly and the teacher handed him the book. He had a big smile on his face when he saw the image of his grandfather.

"Who is that, R.J.?" the teacher asked.

"Granddad," R.J. mumbled. His head was loose on his neck. He seemed to be speaking into his chest.

"That's your grandfather?"

"Grampa," he said, with the slightest bit more power in his voice and a hint of a smile.

"And what did Grandpa do?"

"Sesame," he said.

At least I thought I heard the second word mumbled into his chest.

"That's right, R.J.," his teacher said. "Your grandfather was on *Sesame Street* and he wrote this book, right?"

I couldn't make out what R.J. was saying.

"R.J. Your grandfather wrote this book, right? R.J.?"

He looked up at me and at Holly. The teacher moved the book in front of his face and I could see him struggling to say yes.

"What's your favorite story in this book?"

This was agony for me.

"Hot water," R.J. said. "Lewis."

That's right, the story was about a plumber named Lonesome Lewis.

"Good job, R.J. Thanks for sharing this story with us about the book your grandfather wrote."

As with every other kid, R.J. got healthy applause from the parents who had gathered for this. We were proud of him too. We could see how difficult it was for him to say even that little, with much prompting. But besides the words he said, what we focused on that day was that his eye contact, facial expressions, and speech were so much better than they had been the year before. I knew he was doing really well working hard, and the results were becoming more clear.

When R.J. first enrolled in Smart Start, he didn't even understand that he was in school. The teachers would ask him to walk to the table to start drawing, and he'd just stand there. As we approached the end of his year there, when the teachers told the students to sit at the table, R.J. would be the first one seated, while the other kids still banged on blocks in the corner. He would sit quietly at the table while the teachers rounded up the others.

At home, he sometimes spoke to us spontaneously. I was completely blown away when, after one of our sessions in the park, he said, "Dad, I want French fries." He'd even made some social connections in school. If we kept him in his routine, if he knew the schedule, his meltdowns were mild, short, and infrequent. The day of his presentation, our boy got an A. He had performed better than anyone else in the class.

Still, we believed, he could do even better.

As we noticed the differences between R.J. and his classmates, we began an ongoing conversation with Sharon and the teachers about how to keep pushing him along. We knew it was important to make sure that we were always challenging him, always raising the bar just a fraction of an inch so that he'd need to reach a little farther. One thing we knew we didn't want was for R.J. to be the smartest kid in his class. Holly and I thought there might be such a thing as staying at Smart Start for too long. Some of the older kids seemed stuck. We knew this might be because they were on a different part of the spectrum than R.J. and everything was taking them longer. If what I'd observed was right, R.J. was paying careful attention to the others. We wanted him to have something to which he could aspire: kids who were faster and talked more, who could serve as role models for him.

Smart Start had been so great for R.J. that it was hard to imagine leaving. Khari Lee, one of the other fathers there, described the place as "heaven. How could you leave heaven?" The teachers were so loving to our children and maintained unwavering optimism even when a child's parents might have momentarily fallen into a ditch of hopelessness. But we wanted R.J. to reach for more, and we believed that if we gave him the right kind of support, he just might surprise us all. After six months, we started the ball rolling to get him into a mainstream school.

Ryan was already enrolled in the UCLA Lab School, an elementary school attached to the university's graduate department of education. The school is a place where some of the top scholars in the field can test out their theories of what works in the classroom. In the effort to replicate a typical student body, they accept a student population that reflects the community as a whole. These days, that student body definitely includes children on the autistic spectrum.

While we explored with Sharon whether or not R.J. was ready to leave Smart Start, we were talking to the Lab School about enrolling R.J. in Ryan's class. We spoke to the administrators and the school psychologist. Their attitude was "Bring him!" As long as we hired an aide who would shadow him during the school day and make sure that he was on task and not a burden to the class, R.J. was welcome to enroll. Both he and his sister were happy that they would be together in school again. Yes, it was a leap of faith, but we reasoned that, together as a family, it was a leap we could take.

In reality, I was amazed at how far we all had come in the time since I got past my denial. We were stronger as a family than we had ever been and I was a much better father than I ever could have hoped. I knew who my son was, and I could still say that incredible possibilities were open to him. They might not be the possibilities that I'd imagined for him, and they would definitely take longer for him to achieve, but as far as Holly and I were concerned, they were still limitless.

5

IN THE MAINSTREAM

We had a swimming pool in the backyard of the house we had when the twins were newborns. We had them taking swimming lessons before they could walk. My dad had taught Skip and me to swim before we entered kindergarten, and I believed Ryan and R.J. needed to have that skill mastered even earlier. The pool was a big attraction to them, and we wanted to ensure that they stayed safe.

The swimming teacher who came regularly during the summer before their first birthday was named Conrad. We liked the balance of firmness and enthusiasm that he brought to each lesson. He was big and boisterous, full of life, and the kids were excited too, partly because they wanted to spend more time around him. He taught them basic water safety skills before they were old enough to talk.

The next summer, when the kids could understand his directions better, they learned very quickly that if Conrad told them that he wanted them to do something, they had to do exactly that.

They wouldn't be allowed to progress to the next task until they'd gotten the first one right. Conrad was not the type of guy who would take any mess from anybody. They wanted to please him, so he got them to comply right away.

When I was off for the season, I used to stand in the kitchen and look out the window at the three of them in the pool. R.J. was a sleek little fish, very comfortable in the water and obedient in following directions, whereas Ryan had a tendency to flop around.

"Get to the edge" was Conrad's first order. I'd see R.J. standing right at that edge, but Ryan lingered a step or two back. "Toes lined up on the edge, Ryan." He had the patience to wait and wait until Ryan did as she was instructed. "Big arms! Big arms! No jumping in until I see those big arms!" R.J. hit all Conrad's marker points, followed all his instructions, and jumped right in, while Ryan lagged behind.

Conrad came for an hour a day for two weeks and then took two weeks off. The next session covered more complex skills, building on the techniques they'd learned the last time. Even in R.J.'s deepest dip into autism, he could dive perfectly and move well in the water. He took directions from Conrad and retained the information from one session to the next. He was able to express himself in the pool. As we plunged R.J. into the UCLA Lab School, what was more important to me than his love of the water was the knowledge that, in this at least, R.J. could swim in the mainstream.

The condition the school gave us for allowing R.J. to enroll was that we had to find a full-time aide who could keep him on track throughout the school day. Without one, R.J. probably would be left behind in the classroom unless the teacher devoted more attention to him than she should. The thing about R.J. that made him easy to work with also made him easy to ignore. He didn't cause trouble when he couldn't understand what was going on or if he was overstimulated. He just withdrew. With all the demands on a teacher's attention, R.J. could easily fade into the background. We knew whoever we hired would need to be a miracle worker with a big range of skills and the sensitivity to know just when to intervene and when to hold back. We searched hard until we found the right person to take this job.

In trying to figure out who was right for R.J., we thought that someone with Conrad's basic personality type would be a good fit. The aide needed Conrad's big personality to get R.J.'s attention, but he also had to be focused on R.J. in a way that could give the right mix of challenge and support. Dr. Jeff Jacobs, the Lab School psychologist, cautioned us that a good aide has to be careful not to shrink-wrap himself around the student. The child who is being mainstreamed had to fail from time to time in order to learn; the aide would be doing R.J. a disservice if he didn't allow for those missteps. This aide also had to be charismatic so that the other kids would be interested in being around him. If the aide was un-cool or hovered too much, R.J. wouldn't be able to make friends.

Dr. Jacobs called this concept "scaffolding." The aide is like a strong, light structure around the child that seems barely there, but supports him as he moves gradually higher. And, in addition to all these subtle social and emotional judgments, this aide needed to be a skilled tutor. R.J. definitely would require help on schoolwork outside of class. We couldn't predict how much help he would need. He might catch on quickly and make steady progress as he had at Smart Start. But it was just as likely that he would take a few steps back in a new environment.

We were fortunate to find Mark Kretzmann, who had a degree in speech with a concentration in theater, and had worked with the kids at Smart Start. Speech and theater seemed to be the right combination for R.J. because we expected that Mark would be able to use his gift for expression to help R.J. pay attention at school. Mark is a big guy—more than six feet tall—who makes big movements and can be loud when he needs to be. That theater training gave him the range to be both subtle and responsive.

The other thing we had been working on was R.J.'s diet. R.J. had had so many digestive problems since birth that Holly thought they might indicate that his system was out of whack. This was a problem for many children on the spectrum. Why was it that this child had suffered from diarrhea for most of his life? Holly guessed that he might have food allergies.

We had him tested and discovered that he was allergic to gluten, the protein in wheat flour, which is in just about everything. When a person is allergic to gluten, eating bread can give him intestinal trouble. It may also prevent him from getting the nutrients he needs. In addition, we discovered that R.J. was allergic to casein, the protein in milk, which meant that all dairy products were also off the menu. A casein allergy can mean bloating and stomach cramps when a person eats dairy foods or drinks milk. Many people on the spectrum have these sensitivities. Defeat Autism Now!, one of the organizations Holly got some of her research from, says that some children with autism lack the enzyme that helps them digest these proteins.

R.J. was in pain after almost every meal. Our first pediatrician said he'd grow out of it when his system matured, and he directed us to give R.J. PediaSure for breakfast instead of milk and cereal. For a while, PediaSure was almost the only thing he would eat. We didn't want him to become a picky eater, so we tried to get him to eat other things, but it was very difficult. He either refused and we argued with him, or he got sick. We felt badly about this after we found out about his food allergies. Here we were feeding him all the things healthy kids like, and we were tearing him up from the inside.

Once we received the food allergy report, and cut those foods out of his diet, his diarrhea stopped. He seemed more aware of his environment after that, and he seemed to answer our questions more quickly. That makes sense, of course. How well can you concentrate when your insides are in such turmoil?

Holly also was concerned about the levels of toxins that might have accumulated in R.J.'s system. All of us, even those who keep to a strictly organic diet, pick up some toxic chemicals and metals as we go about eating and breathing in our industrialized world. For the average person exposed to a small amount, the substances enter the body and exit just as quickly. But some autism experts believe that children on the spectrum have a tougher time processing these toxins, which linger in their more sensitive systems, perhaps causing many of their difficult to control behaviors.

Small amounts of mercury, for example, can be found nearly anywhere: in the water system, in old fillings for cavities, and as stabilizers in the vaccines we give to young children. Holly wanted to work in conjunction with a doctor who would help us get rid of those toxins as well as coach us on the right kind of diet for someone with R.J.'s needs. She started working with Dr. Jay Gordon, who had us put R.J. on a chelation regimen to get the toxic metals out of his system. The idea was to give him doses of a substance that contained what they call "sticky molecules," which attract the mercury and other heavy metals. These molecules bind up the toxic metals, and once attached, they pass out of the body.

There are some in the medical community who don't believe this technique is effective. They think that making a child go through this is too hard on his system and, as demonstrated in one well-reported case, has the potential to be fatal. The National Institute of Mental Health in 2008 called off a study of whether or not chelation can help with autism, because they said there wasn't enough evidence supporting its benefits to bother testing the idea.

We tried chelation on R.J. long before the NIMH decision. The idea behind it is that the heavy metals that stabilize and preserve vaccines accumulate in the bodies of a small number of children, the same number who end up on the spectrum. These children have a harder time excreting these toxic elements. Every day we gave R.J. a pill that contained something that these substances would bond with, making it easier for him to eliminate them from his system.

Some parents swore that after a chelation regime, their children had become more responsive, more talkative, and easier to control. Others went so far as to claim that their children had been "cured" by chelation. After seeing how R.J. improved when we eliminated wheat and dairy, which was also controversial in the medical community, we decided that it couldn't do any harm to give chelation a try, under the careful supervision of a doctor. Of all the things we did, this was my least favorite of his therapies. The part that I didn't like had to do with collecting R.J.'s poop.

The doctor said that we couldn't tell if chelation was working unless we sent in a weekly stool sample for testing so that the doctor could determine if R.J. was still excreting toxins. Really? Did we really have to go collect his poop, stuff it in a tube, and send it off in an envelope? I loved to change diapers when the kids were little, but this was much different. I mean, I love that boy more than I can describe, but did we have to go to that extreme to demonstrate it?

Holly said we did. And she reminded me I'd said I would do anything for R.J.

I was kind of hoping she'd forgotten.

Holly joked that she was proud of my commitment to the

cause and was curious as to where I'd found the hazmat suit that I wore for this weekly chore.

Even though this seemed extreme at the time, Holly's unconventional therapies had worked in the past. The problem is that there is no standard treatment for autism. The condition shows up in each kid in a different way. That means that parents who want to really grapple with it had to pull therapies and techniques from everywhere.

As the day approached when R.J. would begin the Lab School, we both noticed that he was looking us in the eye more often and was more vocal in expressing what he wanted to do or eat. His language was stunted, but he could make himself understood, and it was clear that he wanted to be understood, which was big progress. With all the things we were doing to nudge him forward, it was hard to tell how much each of them did to help. One thing was certain, though. We felt that with Mark at his side, and with all the therapies and changes in his diet, we were doing everything we could do. After he made this transition to the Lab School, a lot more of his progress would be up to him.

I think it's important for me to set a baseline here, so that you understand what a leap of faith it was to put R.J. into a regular school. On that first day at the Lab School, it wasn't clear that he knew that he was going to school or if he understood what this new place was about. He knew Smart Start was school, and he had blended into that routine and excelled among those kids. But entering this new world, even with his sister at his side, was confusing. I wished he had the words to tell me how he felt walking into that unfamiliar, crowded, and complicated place.

We had Mark work with R.J. at home the summer before he started at the Lab School so that they would be comfortable with each other. We also wanted to observe them together and make sure that Mark could successfully calm R.J. down and subtly redirect his attention. Mark's other job was to keep him motivated and interested, and make him feel safe.

After the first week of school, we asked Mark to update us, and the news was not good. Mark said that R.J. was having a hard time figuring out where he was and what he was supposed to be doing. Having all these new people around didn't stimulate him. Instead, he shut down.

The basic skills being taught in the classroom were too advanced for R.J., mostly because of his language problems. Dr. Jacobs said that he had expressive and receptive language delays, meaning R.J. had trouble processing all of what you said and calling up the words to respond. Being in a new school, a much bigger one, compounded these problems. Mark had seen R.J. talking spontaneously with us at home, and he said R.J. didn't speak the same way when he was at school. This might have been because, on top of everything else, R.J. seemed anxious. He avoided social contact with Mark and with the other kids. He was withdrawn at recess, walking the perimeter of the yard as he had when he was in the program for two-year-olds at the school that called him "unteachable."

When I looked back to those sessions with Conrad or remembered R.J.'s success at Smart Start, I knew that R.J. wasn't unteach-able. He just had to be taught differently, and Mark was on it.

First he needed to anticipate the schedule. Once R.J. knew what was going to happen during each part of the day, I believed that he'd move through it as easily as he had through the day at Smart Start. Mark was focused on the idea of strength to strength, just as I had been.

Say the kids in his first grade class were on the carpet and the teacher was reading a story about animals in the African jungle. Instead of paying attention, R.J. might be looking off to the side or stimming. The wrong way to get him to focus on the story would be to tell him to pay attention. Mark said that if he got him to do it that way, R.J. would just be following orders. He wouldn't have learned anything about responding to social cues.

Mark believed that the right way to do it was to get in R.J.'s sight lines and give him the most gentle, least restrictive cue by modeling the right behavior. Mark would sit next to him and start reacting a little bit to the story, creating a trail of little bread crumbs that could lead R.J. back to what was happening in the class. If that didn't work, he'd touch him on the shoulder. When R.J. looked up, he'd see Mark using his facial expressions to show R.J. that there was something interesting going on. "Hmm," Mark might say with excited eyes, eyebrows raised and an encouraging smile, when he knew R.J. was looking at him. "Hippos." Mark would guide him to what he should be doing rather than order-ing him to do what everyone else was doing just for the sake of blending in with the rest of class.

Usually, after the teacher read a story, she'd tell the students she wanted them to write a sentence about it. To do this, they would have to get up off the carpet, retrieve their notebooks from their cubbies, and sit down at their desks with pencils in hand.

For R.J., getting his pencil and notebook and making his way to the chair was a process that Mark had to guide him through step-by-step. At each new movement, R.J. would lose focus. Without prompting, he would freeze in the middle of the process while the rest of the students were settling in to do the assignment. As he headed toward the cubbies, Mark had to remind him what he was supposed to get when he got there. At the cubbies, R.J. would be stuck trying to figure out which thing to get. In the beginning, Mark had to prompt him three or four times at each step along the way.

After trying to guide him through that process a few times, Mark decided he would set the pencil and the notebook at the table for R.J. That task was less important than the work of retaining the story, figuring out what to write, and the difficult physical act of putting pencil to paper. Unless Mark did the setup, by the time R.J. got to the table and was ready to try to write, the other kids would be almost finished.

Despite what Mark told us about how jarring this transition was for R.J., I never gave up hope. We had detached our expectations from a timetable—this is the first lesson all parents of children with autism have to learn—but we wanted him to have something to reach for, and I trusted that he would attain his

goals as soon as he got oriented. We knew that in certain con-
texts, such as swimming with Conrad, he could follow directions, but he had a harder time in others. When the waters were
calm for R.J., he knew how to move through them. For the first
few months at the Lab School, the waters were rough, and R.J.
couldn't navigate as well as the other kids. My hope—well, my
near certainty—was that, over time, he would reach in and find
those skills and understand how to apply them at school.

It's true that there were times during that first year when
Holly and I wondered if we had made the right decision placing
R.J. in the Lab School. Smart Start had been a wonderful, safe
place where they cradled the kids and allowed them to make
gentle progress at their own pace. Was the Lab School too much
for R.J.? Had we moved him too soon? Had we asked so much of
him that we were going to make him regress? Those are the kinds
of questions that parents always torture themselves with when
their children are struggling. Mark reminded us, as did all of R.J.'s
team of therapists, that everyone had to put in hours with R.J. to
make tiny gains, almost imperceptible gains, every day. We had
to give this change more time.

Every afternoon, Mark came home from school with the twins
and helped them do their homework. This was where Mark
and R.J. would really focus on his work at school. Mark could be
tougher on him at home than he was at school, where the other
kids would see Mark's one-on-one tutoring.

At home, R.J. acted like any other kid who didn't want to do his
homework. Many kids on the spectrum can't sit still, but R.J.

would never run away. When I saw Mark working with R.J., I could see R.J. get tired and frustrated. By watching Mark, I learned the subtle way he gauged how to always keep R.J. in the intermediate difficulty zone: careful not to give him something that was too far out of his reach. If the work got hard and R.J. seemed tired, Mark would dial it back a bit.

The first grade seemed to be all about getting R.J. familiar with the Lab School routine, getting him set up with a few friends, and getting him comfortable with the structure so that he could relax and learn better. By the end of the first year, we had a much better understanding of how his mind worked and what his strengths were. He has a great visual memory and a strong sense of spatial skills. That brain of his is a steel trap for facts. Things that are ordered and predictable are extremely satisfying to him. As the second grade began, we all agreed that now that he had adapted to the new routine, the focus should be on trying to get him up to speed in math and reading. As hard as R.J. was working, the truth was that his reading and math weren't coming along very well.

R.J. had a great teacher in the second grade, Deanna Staake, who in the classroom had created her own safe place for the kids that they all came to call the Tree House. Two walls of the room where the books were stored were all glass and nestled close up against a beautiful mature magnolia tree. When the kids sat there as a group for reading, or retreated there to pick out books to read on their own, it felt like they were escaping into the filtered light and shadows of a secret tree house.

Deanna understood our goals for R.J. and tried to call on him during every discussion. Part of her teaching philosophy was that the classroom was a place where everyone was recognized for his or her strengths and weaknesses and everyone had something to contribute. I loved the fact that she talked about this right up front and challenged all the kids to think about themselves and the kids around them. One of the things that Deanna's community-building in the classroom touched off in R.J. was thoughts about what it was that was different about him.

As a result of this, Holly and I ended up having another discussion with him about autism. We'd talked to him about it before, but all the therapists recommended that we revisit the subject every few years when we thought he might be able to take in a little bit more information. We had explained how he saw things differently and felt things differently, but it wasn't clear that R.J. could understand his differences even with those simple descriptions. This time we talked about how his brain worked in a way that made him special.

Mark incorporated this into his work with R.J. and began to show him the book we got with pictures of famous people from history who some historians suspect may have had autism. The list includes Albert Einstein, Vincent van Gogh, Mozart, Andy Warhol, and somebody R.J. could definitely identify: Jim Henson, the creator of the Muppets his grandfather hung out with on *Sesame Street*.

Mark did a great job of showing R.J. the paintings these artists had created and playing pieces of music written by these composers. Illustrating how R.J. was special by appealing to his senses was a way to get around the cascade of words that sometimes was overwhelming for R.J. This information stuck with R.J. He began to understand that whatever problems this caused him now, autism wasn't necessarily a deficit. He would ask Mark to show him these paintings and play these songs again and again.

This was a nice turning point for R.J., we thought. And maybe it was bigger than we knew. He was trying to put the pieces of himself together to make an identity. This is a basic struggle for anyone to take on, particularly daunting for someone as young as R.J. Most kids struggle with their place in the social pecking order. I know R.J. was doing that too. But in addition to that, he also had to figure out why his world operated on a different timetable than everyone else's. If he could find a way to see that as an advantage, we were making good progress.

Meanwhile Mark was working laboriously with him on reading and math, a plodding process where that incremental progress was barely detectable. It seemed like R.J. would never be able to read a full sentence without being coached, and he had terrible trouble adding numbers for a sum greater than twenty. He would start to add, but it took him a long time to get reliable once the numbers were larger than he could count on his fingers. Then Mark tried pretzels, which he lined up like little soldiers in groups of ten on the kitchen table. He'd have R.J. count them out as he did a math problem, but as soon as the pretzels were allocated, the idea behind the way they had been arranged was gone, just a wisp of an idea that had flown out of his mind.

I was frustrated for him because I believed that the certain world of numbers was a place where he could succeed if he could just get the basic concepts down. Even when Mark was not working with him, I'd try to slip in a few math games in order to add another layer of reinforcement, just as I had that day kicking the ball in the park.

One afternoon, Holly and I were upstairs when we heard all kinds of shouts and commotion coming from the kitchen table where Mark and R.J. were laboring over his homework. Then we heard an excited yell of "Mom! Dad! Dad! Dad!" Then we felt the sound of R.J. running up the stairs with the heavy pounding of Mark right behind. R.J. threw open the door to our bedroom without knocking, something he had always been cautioned not to do. But with that look on his face, how could I take this moment to remind him?

"Watch," R.J. said breathlessly.

"What's eight plus six?" Mark asked, a big grin on his face.

"Eight in my head," said R.J. touching his skull to place the number in his head. "Six on the hand. Nine, ten, eleven, twelve, thirteen, fourteen. Fourteen!"

Holly and I stood there with our mouths open.

Mark continued. "Okay, R.J. What's seven plus nine?"

"Nine." He pounded on the side of his head as his smile got bigger. Then he placed his hands before him and ticked off each number as he shouted it out. "Ten, eleven, twelve, thirteen, fourteen, fifteen, sixteen. Sixteen! Sixteen!"

I don't think I could have been prouder of R.J. if he had written a symphony. He had been working on this with Mark for nearly two years. And while he might whine and try to get out of it like any other kid would, he'd kept at it. When Mark found the magic trick, R.J. just ran with it.

Although they had been working on reading and writing without success in the same laborious way, shortly after this head-pounding breakthrough, R.J. started to read and write in a much different way.

At first, when Mark started working with R.J. on reading, he couldn't read even a short page in a simple children's book all the way through. He could pick out a few words, but not a whole sentence. Mark was constantly on the hunt for books that might interest him at his reading level. When he was in second grade, he introduced these very simple books about a boy and his 180-pound dog called *Henry and Mudge.*

There must be nearly a hundred of these books. One of the good things about the series is that they are designed to bring the kids along at increasing levels of difficulty. They start out at pre-reading with basic words that the kids can pick out. Then they move forward to reading the most simple sentences. The series continues on in this way until the end, when the children are prepared to read the last books in the series on their own.

The books use the same words—like dog and boy—over and over, giving the young reader something to recognize and be successful with. They also feature very simple stories. Henry and Mudge go to the beach and dig a hole. The end. As he and Mark worked up to the next level of the series, R.J. could finish a book then move on to the next one, which had the same characters and a similarly simple story, giving him a sense of mastery. Deanna's system for getting the kids to read was also ingenious. Each student had a box to store the books the student was reading and another for the books he or she planned to read next. R.J. really hit his stride as he filled his boxes with those books.

The rest of the students were reading a different series, which was appropriately called *The Magic Tree House* series. In the beginning, those books, which are more than a hundred pages long, were too tough for R.J. to handle. But that tree house was the place he wanted to be. The idea behind the series was that the kids, Jack and Annie, enter a tree house that has a library through which they are able to go back in time to any period of history or to any part of the earth they want to visit. Through the tree house, they could go to Egypt or see the knights and castles of the Middle Ages, go into space or deep into the sea. R.J. wanted to be reading those books like everyone else, so this gave him something to work toward.

By Valentine's Day of second grade, all of these skills that he had worked so hard to master were coming together. The most important piece, and the one that brought all of this together, was the social piece. He had started playing handball with the kids at recess and was getting pretty good at it. R.J. was also on the soccer team. He had a few friends and some playdates. Then he took on a task that surprised all of us.

As Valentine's Day approached, Deanna laid down some

ground rules for how to give classmates valentines. She said each student had to give everyone in the class a valentine, and none of them could be those store-bought ones that capitalize on the latest animation craze. The kids had to make them. That alone would have been a huge task for R.J., but in addition, he told us that he wanted to write something personal on each one.

Part of us wanted to ask R.J. if he was sure he wanted to do this. Writing was still a very difficult and time-consuming task for him. But this ambition of personalizing each card showed how much he wanted to express his affection for the other students in the class and was a demonstration of his good heart. And R.J. was determined.

We realized he could only do a few of them at a time, maybe three a day at most. Every day, as part of his homework, he and Mark sat together and began by deciding what very simple sentence he wanted to write to one of his classmates. After they'd decided on that sentence, R.J. would put together a Valentine from the red and white hearts and stickers Holly had bought. Then R.J. painstakingly wrote out the sentence. Each one of these writing assignments took a half an hour or more. He'd have to take a break between finishing one and starting the next. If he seemed to have the energy after dinner, we might get him to do one more.

There were twenty-four kids in the class, plus Deanna and the two aides. This meant that we couldn't let up on the production schedule. I was so proud of R.J. for thinking up this idea and keeping at it. While the other kids might not have noticed how much love R.J. put into these little cards, we did and so did Ms.

Staake. On hers he wrote, "Ms. Staake you are always nice to everybody. Love Rodney." She still has that valentine.

So this kid, who supposedly would never look us in the eye and never say "I love you" unprompted, had a sophisticated notion of the differences among the kids in his class, along with a need to tell them how much he thought of them. Not only that, he was also willing to put in the enormous amount of work it took for him to express it.

Mark picked up on how important this Valentine's Day triumph was for R.J. He knew that when we saw something that R.J. wanted to do, we should look for a way to work some of the other skills he was trying to master into that activity. In making those valentines, R.J. used his talent for spatial relations in designing the cards. He also wanted more friends, so he did something to please them, which meant he had to think and to write something nice about each one of them. Mark, seeing this need for expression, found a new area where R.J. could excel.

Afternoons at home, when R.J. took a break before he and Mark got down to homework, R.J. would frequently sit in front of the baby grand piano we had in the living room and plunk around on the keys. Holly had taught him a few simple songs and Mark had taught him "Heart and Soul." As he got to the end of the third-grade year, Mark saw that R.J. was sitting at the piano more and more. Why not try to teach him to read music?

The advantage of reading music over reading words is that music is consistent. The rules that govern the notes always apply, unlike when R.J. was trying to sound out the crazy phonics of

English. R.J. appeared to have some natural talent in music and he was drawn to it. Within weeks of beginning lessons with Mark, he could read bass and treble clefs and could use both hands to play simple pieces. Holly would hear them on the piano and come rushing down with joy to sing along with R.J.

Eventually we got R.J. a music teacher who specialized in teaching children with autism. When we first met him, he proudly proclaimed that he never taught his students to read music because that just complicated things. Then Mark produced one of the elementary music books he'd been using to teach R.J. The new teacher looked on amazed as R.J. played the song. Who could blame him? We were all more than a little amazed by R.J.

March is the Nickelodeon Kids' Choice Awards, an event that most kids would beg and plead to attend. We'd had a number of disasters there, with R.J. screaming and having to be taken out, but we refused to leave him at home. The previous year we'd asked his therapists to help us figure out how to soothe R.J. in a scene like this: a stadium full of loud noises, screaming crowds—and, because it was Nickelodeon, buckets of slime. If you could design a torture chamber for kids on the spectrum, those would be the elements to include.

The previous year, the therapists had trained us to massage R.J.'s body when he started to melt down. Holly and I were supposed to take him to a corner where the noise wasn't so overwhelming and rub his limbs while talking to him in soothing voices. This technique was supposed to re-center him on his body so that he could begin to handle all the external stimulation that this event would throw at him. It worked for a while, but we had to cut our time there short when R.J. reached his limit.

As with everything else we did with R.J., we never gave up hope that over time he would be able to take it all in. So even though we had some hesitation about bringing him, we decided once again that we would attend the awards as a family. On the way over to the stadium, I thought about R.J. and all the progress he had been making. Even before he was born, I imagined our relationship like something out of *Father Knows Best*. But as we drove, I realized that my actual highlight reel was much less conventional and far more precious to me than anything Hollywood could have dreamed up: R.J. playing handball and beating me as we played against the garage door; him working hour after hour at the kitchen table to create those heartfelt valentines; the joy on his face as he slapped the math solutions into his head; reading a book of more than a hundred pages on his own in the tree house; playing songs on the piano; and lastly, planting his feet firmly on the linoleum in front of his class as he told a complicated story about a time he was scared but everything came out fine in the end.

All those events in the last year were huge victories for R.J. and for us. They were moments that we'd never thought were possible, when he could be just like a normal kid in so many ways.

We parked the car and walked toward the stadium entrance, hearing the roar of the cheering crowd and the noise of the sound system. I looked over at R.J. He didn't appear to be scared.

"You know who is going to be there tonight? SpongeBob!"

"Yeah!"

"That's your favorite. He's going to come out a little while after we take our seats," I said.

We entered the arena and the place was in chaos. I had R.J. by the hand as we found where we were supposed to sit. The floor was vibrating from the noise, the kind of noise that is layers of sound: the band, the cheering, the sound effects, the screaming of the kids behind us. *I* felt like freaking out. I looked down at R.J., who seemed a little agitated. He was looking around frantically, squirming in his seat. He looked up at me to express his concern.

"Dad, when will SpongeBob get here?"

"Soon. He'll be right out."

That was it. There we were, right in the center of the mainstream.

6

YOU DO THE MATH

I paced around in the family room as R.J. sat on the sofa. His presentation to the fifth-grade class about the state of Michigan was the next day and he didn't seem to care. At least he didn't appear to be as concerned about it as I was. This was a big deal. He had to report about the history, economy, and culture of a state, in front of all of his classmates and their parents. He could remember facts well, but standing up before an audience and projecting his voice so everyone could hear him had always been difficult for him.

We had put together a big board covered with pictures of the things he was going to talk about, so there would be something to cue him during the presentation. He would also have to speak into a microphone. There would most likely be about fifty people in that room and I didn't want him to embarrass himself. From the attitude I was getting from him, with his body slumped and a look of total boredom on his face, it appeared to me that he didn't care how this came off.

"The capital of Michigan is what?" I asked him.

He looked like he was napping, or about to be.

"I did this with Tim this afternoon," he said.

"Tell me what the capital of Michigan is," I insisted.

"Lansing," he mumbled.

"What did you just say? You've got to speak up. This is a big presentation," I said.

"Lansing," he said, just a little bit louder.

"What do they make in Michigan?"

"Cars," he said.

"What kind of cars? Who started making cars in Michigan?"

"Ford."

"When you say that, you've got to point to the board here so they have a picture to go with the kind of car. Which one of these pictures are you going to point to when you say that?"

He lifted up his arm and weakly pointed in the direction of the board, not indicating any particular corner.

"Come on, R.J., you can do better than that!"

"We did this in school," he said. "I don't want to do this."

I wanted him to understand how important it was for him to get it right, but he wasn't having any of it. This was one of those moments when the big picture of what I wanted for him and the smaller picture of what he wanted to do with his evening were in conflict. If I kept reminding him that he was going to be standing in front of all those parents and their video cameras when he gave this presentation, emphasizing that this might scare him, he might respond by just shutting down.

Honestly, I was the one who didn't want to be embarrassed. R.J. had come incredibly far in the five years we had him at the Lab School. This was a moment when he could shine, if he felt like it.

When fourth grade began, we'd had to hire him a new aide. Mark Kretzmann was so well trained and so intuitive when it came to working with R.J. that the staff at the school had taken notice of his skills. There were several special needs students there who had full-time aides, but some of those aides weren't very effective. It was clear to everyone that Mark had a special touch.

The research arm of the school had developed a way to assess the aides' techniques and the results they got with the students. When Mark scored the highest on this scale, getting 90 percent, they invited him to enroll in UCLA to get his master's in special education. We were sad to see him go, but so happy for him that this new chapter was opening in his life. Through this study, maybe he could help train a whole generation of aides who would be as helpful to their kids as he had been to R.J.

We were fortunate that Tim Lee, a young man who was working with another child with autism at the Lab School, had completed his work with that family. Tim was smaller in stature than Mark, but he was charismatic and expressive in his own way. I liked that he was a fanatic about professional sports, an interest that R.J. and I shared. Just like when Mark started with us, we had Tim work at home with R.J. during the summer so they would be familiar with each other by the time school started.

I could see the two of them out on the pavement near the garage where I had set up a basketball hoop for R.J. Ever since he was very small, one of R.J.'s ways of handling the times when he felt overwhelmed was to dribble a basketball. We always let him do this for a half an hour a day. We thought of it as his time, a time to relax. After that half hour was up, we cut it off. If we let it go on for too long, it would become a retreat. But R.J. also had a natural bounce in his step, his hop, that made us think he might end up being a pretty good player when the time came for him to play organized basketball. With everything else that filled R.J.'s day, though, we never spent too much time on hoops.

Tim was getting to know R.J. by trying to teach him how to shoot baskets. I could see it was tough going at first. R.J. only wanted to dribble the ball, because that was in his comfort zone. Tim showed R.J. the proper form for shooting a basket. He shot a few, then gave the ball to R.J., who still just wanted to dribble. Tim stopped him and worked on positioning R.J.'s arms the right way to make a free throw.

R.J. had a hard time performing the movements in sequence and letting go of the ball at the right moment. Tim was so patient. R.J. never made a basket during the first hour they spent on this, and most of his shots weren't even close. But Tim just kept adjusting R.J.'s arms and counting off the sequence. He never got rattled. As I watched them in the month before school started, I again felt so lucky that we'd found another smart, talented, and good-hearted person to work with R.J.

Tim's instincts were similar to Mark's in believing that R.J. needed a light touch on the academic work at school and more aggressive tutoring at home. During the school day, R.J. needed to be part of the gang, not the guy with an aide hovering over him. Fourth grade was so much harder than third. Fourth is the grade when the teachers really start to pile on the work and demand that students perform a higher order of thinking. They want them to draw information from a variety of sources and make reports. English class is harder too. There are fewer pictures in the books, and for the most advanced readers, there are no pictures at all. In math, the numbers are larger and the concepts are more abstract. Abstract thought was hard for R.J. We believed Tim would have his work cut out for him by trying to keep R.J. current on these more sophisticated subjects.

Then something new started happening with R.J.: he wanted to learn.

Maybe he had wanted to learn all along, but everything had initially been so overwhelming that he was doing all he could to keep up with the basics. As Tim began working with him over the summer, they focused on basic single-digit multiplication. This was easy stuff for someone with such a good mind for facts. Three times three is always going to be nine. Tim said R.J. understood single-digit multiplication right from the beginning. About two weeks into these lessons, R.J. said he wanted to try multiplying three digits.

At first, Tim resisted a little. We told him that slow and steady had always been the right approach with R.J., but R.J. kept saying, "I can do it. I can do it. Just teach me." Tim thought, *Who am I to hold him back?* He created a sheet of three-digit multiplication problems for R.J., who was excited to give them a try. He got all of them wrong on the first pass, but his enthusiasm was still strong. He wanted to keep trying because he knew he could get it right.

One day when Tim was again going over the basic concepts, he put his finger down on the page to show R.J. how to align the numbers to get the correct answer, and R.J. moved his finger away. "I got it," he said. "I got it."

And he did.

This was a huge change for him: initiating learning. He has pride in what he does and what he can do, but he had claimed that he hated school. The challenge was to motivate him to do well in the schoolroom. This was exactly the problem we were having with this presentation about the great state of Michigan.

"What's the state bird, R.J.?"

Silence from the couch.

"R.J., what is the state bird of Michigan?"

Mumble, mumble.

What was this? The normal grumpy reaction of a tired pre-teen? Or a slip backward?

"Speak up! Speak up!"

Mumble.

"The bird?"

"The robin."

"Right!"

I beamed at him, trying to get him enthused, but he was giving me that same grumpy look.

Where was R.J. on the spectrum now? It was halfway through

the school year. Tim said that R.J. was, in his way, now a self-starter in class. When he came into the classroom at the beginning of the day, Tim no longer had to prompt him to look on the chalkboard to figure out what materials he had to get out for the first assignment. He did the same thing as the others: read the board, set up, and sit down. In this context, he had independence. Holly and I had spoken to his class about autism earlier in the year, and he was invited to more playdates than he had been in the past

Inside the class there were two kids who looked after R.J., and his teacher, Julie Kern, said that when you saw him with them, it was hard to believe there was any difference among them, that R.J. was a child with autism. In the beginning of the school year, there was a little bit of jostling about who would be allowed to sit next to R.J. in class. Mrs. Kern chose a boy and a girl because, between them, they were the right combination of helpers.

The boy looked after R.J., but in a guy's kind of way. Mrs. Kern's class was a talkative one. Not an hour went by without some interaction. When she prompted the class to do something, R.J. frequently needed to hear that more than once. With the boy next to him, he got called out by his friend. "Get yourself together, Rodney. You're supposed to have your pencil when you come over here," the boy would say. And the girl is the kind of friend who would just get the pencil for him.

Not only had he figured out who his friends were, he'd identified a few kids he *didn't* like. One day in the yard, one of the kids, a guy who had a bit of a temper, got on R.J.'s nerves and R.J.

pushed him. The kid fell to the ground. Tim was standing at the sidelines thinking that he should stop this, but he paused. He realized that it was okay for R.J. to know that there was a child out there he didn't like.

After a moment, Tim pulled R.J. aside and told him that it was okay that he didn't like everyone and that there would always be a few people he didn't get along with. His job, Tim told him, was to work it out or keep his distance.

"What do you want to do?" Tim asked him.

"I'll stay away," R.J. said.

The part of R.J.'s progress that Holly treasured the most was a story Tim told her about a day that he came to school very sick, coughing and miserable. R.J. came up to him and asked, "Are you okay?" Tim admitted that he wasn't feeling well. R.J. patted him on the back and told him that he should go home. R.J. said he would be able to do the school day without him. He was sensitive to Tim and could see he was hurting. He had empathy for that. Empathy, compassion, and an ability to read the physical state of another person were characteristics that we had been told R.J. would never grasp.

Over this past school year, he'd been having spontaneous interactions and initiating conversations with other kids. In math he was asking to learn more and told us that he didn't need as much help as we thought he did. He was making significant demands on himself. The fact that he was integrated into the school and having spontaneous contacts was so much beyond where the specialists had predicted he would be when he entered the Lab School two years earlier. He had even exceeded the hopes that I had had for him when he first started there. As Tim said, "I will never say never with Rodney. He surprises me all the time."

His report card, though, was not a pleasant surprise. The school's grading system ranked student performance by numbers one through three, with one the lowest. Two meant the student wasn't meeting grade-level expectations but could perform tasks without support. On his report cards, R.J. got twos straight down the line. Was this the way it had to be? This is a territory in which parents of children on the spectrum are stuck too. Should we have been content that he was getting what equaled an average grade in a regular classroom? Or were we at one of those junctures with him where if we pushed him just the right amount and gave him just the right support, he could break through to a new level?

I looked at the young man sprawled over the couch. He didn't appear at the moment to be preparing to scale new heights.

"R.J., the state flower of Michigan is what?"

He wasn't even listening. Had he fallen asleep?

"What's the state flower of Michigan, R.J.? There's a picture of it right here on the board."

"The apple blossom."

"Right! And why is that? Why is the state flower of Michigan the apple blossom."

"They grow apples."

"How many?"

That was a question guaranteed not to get a response.

"Dad, I did this at school."

"Then you should know the answer."

"Michigan grows apples."

I could feel the anxiety building in me, as it did each time R.J. had to stand in front of the class and present something. These were the moments when the differences between him and his peers were plain for all to see. All the other kids were going to grab the mike and say, "My state is Oklahoma and the capital is Oklahoma City and . . ." It didn't have to be this way. His public performances had gotten better every year, but they still required a lot of effort on everyone's part. I remember him being frustrated during the other times he'd had to present to the class, and not being able to read the words right. Mark had had to stand up there with him and prompt him to read the next word. The way he was acting, I didn't believe he was going to show any improvement tomorrow. If he didn't take this seriously, he was going to stand up there and mumble. If he would just put in a little effort now, it wouldn't have to be that way this time.

The next morning, on the way to the school presentation, I did something I wasn't supposed to do. I slipped R.J. a stick of gum. Gum is forbidden at school, but it can be useful for kids on the spectrum. The rhythm of chewing calms them down and helps them to shut out the distractions of the world.

When we entered the classroom, it was jammed with parents standing along the wall at the back, many of them with video cameras at their sides. When Mrs. Kern called on R.J., Holly got him to take the gum out of his mouth and put it in a tissue before he took the podium.

With that microphone in his hand, he was a rock star. He moved around like he'd been doing this all his life: the professor giving his yearly lecture on Michigan, the Great Lakes, the upper and lower peninsulas, cars, apples, minerals, the whole nine. The fact that it was so effortless for him blew everyone away. Half the parents in the room had known R.J. since he first started at this school and had the videotape of those mumbled, overly prompted presentations. He got hearty applause even before he started taking questions from the audience. He was so comfortable and easy with it.

And I had been so afraid for him. I had been fussing over him and anxious—too anxious to believe him when he said, "I practiced this a million times. I got it."

Never say never with R.J.

R.J., out in the world and handling things on his own, had to be the next goal for him and for us as a family.

We sold our house shortly before the school year ended in 2009. While we were looking for another, we rented a big townhouse right in the middle of Westwood, the commercial area at the southern end of UCLA. The kids loved that we could just walk out the front door and be in the middle of a city street scene instead of having to drive everywhere. There was a sandwich shop across the street, coffee bars, fast food, ice cream, music, and street life everywhere. This set a perfect stage for teaching R.J. how to handle the world on his own.

The abstract math that the kids were studying in fifth grade was a huge source of tension and frustration to R.J. But we believed that he could be functional in the ways that you need to use math in everyday life—the kind of math you need to make sure that the store clerk has given you the right change.

After we were sure that he was well oriented in the neighborhood and could guide the group of us back to the entrance to the condo, we started giving him small errands to do. We'd give him a twenty-dollar bill and send him across the street to the Trader Joe's to get some items for dinner, or over to the drugstore to pick out a snack. His job was to buy whatever we told him to buy with that twenty, nothing more, and make sure that he got the proper change. When he got home, we asked him for the receipt so we could check his math.

Parents of special needs children can appreciate the panic Holly and I experienced sending R.J. across the street alone with money in his hand. We handed him the key to the apartment and the twenty and kissed him like he was going off to climb Mount Everest. Then we stood at the window with our hearts beating in our throats as he waited to cross the street, which he did casually, not reflecting any of the anxiety that his parents were swallowing. Then he came back. No big deal. We could tell how happy he was to be granted this bit of independence.

Each time we sent him out, we lengthened the leash a little bit more. At the beginning of the summer break, we decided he'd proven to be reliable enough that we'd chance letting him and his little brother, Robinson, go out together. They'd both been great kids all school year. Robinson's grades were excellent and R.J. was holding his own. He showed consistent effort and a desire to learn while accepting support from Tim. As the school year was winding down, both of the boys had really enjoyed watching the Lakers win the NBA championship. Holly and I decided a nice reward for them would be to let them buy Lakers gear. We agreed that he and Robinson could buy shirts at a store around the corner from our place. I handed R.J. two twenties and they went forth on their mission.

Half an hour later, they came back screaming at each other, R.J. on the verge of tears, and with only a T-shirt for Robinson in the bag. We talked to them for almost half an hour before we figured out what had happened.

Robinson picked out a shirt that came in just under twenty dollars while R.J.'s cost twenty-two. When R.J. saw the final price on the cash register, he blew up at Robinson for spending too much money. Robinson argued with him. He knew the shirt that he'd chosen did not go over budget. R.J. didn't want to hear any of this from his little brother and they got into it at the store. In the end, R.J. bought his brother's shirt and came home without one of his own, scowling and berating Robinson all the way.

I sat with R.J., trying to calm him down. He was furious and embarrassed. He blamed Robinson. He blamed me for not giving him enough money. The solution to this was to show him the math.

I took out the receipt and the change he had returned to me so we could look at the numbers. The world of numbers was a place where we could settle this, because numbers are not emotions. They were not embarrassing, and didn't blame anyone. We added up how much his shirt cost and how much Robinson's had cost to show him that starting out with something that cost twenty-two dollars meant that Robinson was going to get the short end of the stick. I complimented him on doing the right thing, the big brother thing, and letting his little brother get his shirt instead of deciding to get the one he'd chosen.

"R.J., you did the right thing with the shirts, but verbally attacking your brother in the store is unacceptable," I said. "When you saw you didn't have enough money, how much more did you need?"

"About five dollars," he said.

"So the right thing to do was to come back here and get that five dollars, wasn't it?" I asked.

"I thought Robinson was spending too much money," R.J. said.

"But he wasn't. His shirt was less than twenty dollars," I said. "You did the right thing. You didn't let it go to the point where no one got anything. That was a good decision. What's the right thing to do now?"

"Go back to the store," he said, his head hung low in embarrassment.

"Just to buy the shirt, is that why you want to go back?" I asked.

"No, I want to talk to the lady," he said.

"What do you want to talk to her about?" I said.

"I want to apologize," R.J. said. "I apologize to her and I apologize to Robinson. I'm sorry, Robinson. I shouldn't have yelled at you in the store."

"It's okay," Robinson said. "I accept your apology."

"I'm sorry to you, Dad," R.J. continued. "I shouldn't have blamed you and Mom for not giving me enough money. I should know."

All the way on the walk back to the store R.J. and I talked the math of money and how to handle money, and how to act if you find you don't have enough. I thought there was a lesson in this for him about how to handle a conflict like this the right way, but I wasn't sure what lesson he would take from it.

When we got to the store, I stood outside while he went in to apologize for making a scene. When he came back out to join me, the manager was with him. She told us that she appreciated the fact that he returned to apologize. She respected how hard that was for him. "So few children do that," she said. "You are a very nice young man." She nodded knowingly at me, parent-to-parent, and went back into the store.

We headed back home. R.J. had a very serious look on his face. "I think I learned a lesson, Dad," he said. "This was a lesson."

"What lesson do you take from this?"

"I have to get better at math," he said.

This was true, but it was also true that he was getting better at calculating his place in the world, and understanding how to size things up. I knew that when it came to the important things, R.J. could do the math.

7

EPILOGUE

Singing His Song

People who don't have a close relationship with children who have autism tend to make assumptions about them. One of the most common ones is that children on the spectrum are happy being alone. People may watch them, moving around in a rhythmic way with sly smiles on their faces as they talk to themselves, and think that they seem content. When you try to talk to some of these children, they might push you away, seeming to prefer being on their own. Yet we never really know what they think or how they feel, because many of them cannot express themselves except in times of fear or frustration.

Mark Kretzmann, R.J.'s first aide, who is now in graduate school studying autism, told me about a study undertaken by researchers that was meant to determine if children with autism were more likely to suffer from loneliness. The researchers asked both typical kids and kids on the spectrum about their feelings of loneliness when they looked back to their time in elementary school. The study found that both groups of children had equal feelings of isolation. Just as many typical kids had trouble connecting with others and expressing their feelings as kids on the spectrum.

We have a friend in Los Angeles, Elaine Hall, who is the woman who founded the Miracle Project, a theater group for kids on the spectrum that was focal point of the documentary *Autism, The Musical*. People hear that title and they start grinning. The idea that these kids—most of whom have trouble stringing a sentence together, let alone performing in front of a huge audience—could get up and perform a whole musical just seems crazy. I admit that when I first heard about it, I thought it would be difficult to organize. But Elaine pulls it off. And it's become such an important program for the children and their families who are involved. Many parents like us use almost every activity as another route to finding some way to express how their children feel. So Elaine thought, *Why not also use music and theater to reach out to our children and pull them into our world?*

As you know from reading this book, we tried everything we could to reach R.J. We used anything he showed the smallest flicker of interest in (and several things that didn't interest him at all) to give him a new mode of expression: sports, music, video games, animals. When Holly and Elaine met, they focused on the musical aspect. They were interested in getting well-known music producers and performers from different genres to work with some of our kids to produce an album that could raise money to support services for children on the spectrum.

The first great matchup was with Wyatt Stills, whose dad is Stephen Stills. Wyatt did a song with Jack Black that turned out very well. This gave Holly the idea of trying to work on a song with R.J.

Although Holly is a fine singer, she'd never worked on original material before. She searched out Kenneth "Babyface" Edmonds, who is a friend of ours, hoping that she could convince him to donate a little bit of his time to work on a song with her and R.J. No doubt, he's a very busy man, but he was interested in the idea.

"Send me the lyrics and I'll see what I can do," he told Holly.

"Oh, you want *me* to write the lyrics? I thought you were going to write the song," Holly said.

"Holly, I don't have a kid with autism. How am I supposed to write a song about that? When you think about R.J. and autism, what do you want to say?" Kenny asked.

"I think about loneliness and how these kids are misunderstood," she responded.

"That sounds like a good place to start. Write something and send it to me," he said, and he hung up.

Good things sometimes come from being under pressure. And Holly was feeling the pressure. I mean, here was Babyface Edmonds ready to produce her very first song. She sat down and thought about what it would be like to be inside R.J.'s world and what he would try to show her if he could bring her in. The song came out very fast, and I think it's beautiful.

COME INTO MY WORLD

Come into my world
Then you will see
I am just like u
S'hard to be me

Open your mind
Open your heart
I want to know u
I'm beggin u please?

Come into my world . . .

So many moments, so many times
I wanna talk to u
just wanna vibe with u

Want you to know me, too much to share . . .
How can I reach for u . . . ?
so that it's just us two

So much frustration limiting
the possibilities
to
show u

And when silence steals the space I meant for imprisoned words
please know that

I'm
Still
There

Come into my world
Then u will see
This don't define me
S'much more to me

Look into my eyes
It's where I live
Connect to the love, babe
So much to give

Come into my world

Come into my world

Come into my world

Holly thought that writing up the lyrics would be the end of her work, until Kenny told her to sing the song as she heard it in her head into a digital tape recorder, then upload it as a file and send it to him.

She knew this was way beyond her level of technical expertise. Whenever you're in doubt about technology, ask a child. Ryan did it for her.

R.J., Robinson, and Ryan hanging out with me on the sidelines at a Carolina Panthers game in 2004
Holly Robinson Peete

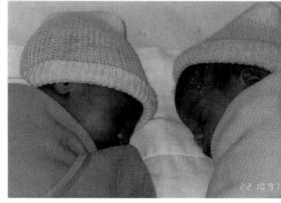

The twins, five days old
Holly Robinson Peete

R.J.'s first football game, age two, when I played for the Redskins *Holly Robinson Peete*

R.J.'s big catch, and smile for our approval *Holly Robinson Peete*

I don't know of a more beautiful pregnant woman   *Alex Berliner*

Above Left: The twins at six months. Notice how Ryan struggles to hold up her head.   *Holly Robinson Peete*

Below Left: R.J. always has had a connection to animals
    Holly Robinson Peete

The whole family before Roman, 2003, R.J., Ryan, Holly, Robinson, and me
    Ronna Shary

Mom and son, age eight, back-to-school night   *Rodney Peete*

R.J. and me in Hawaii, 2001   *Holly Robinson Peete*

R.J. slam dunk   *Holly Robinson Peete*

R.J. with his devilish smile, age five   *Holly Robinson Peete*

Family photo day outside the
Peete home in LA
Donyell McCullough

My boy, the fish,
in Hawaii
Holly Robinson Peete

R.J. and Robinson in South Africa
at the opening of the Oprah
Winfrey School
Holly Robinson Peete

R.J. showing his affection for animals,
November 2008, in the Bahamas
Holly Robinson Peete

R.J. and Robinson trying not to
get wet as they leap around a
river outside Atlanta   *Boris Kodjoe*

Above: Holly and I renew our vows
at the Wynn Hotel on our ten-year
anniversary. This time, we do it
with all the kids.   *Dolores Robinson*

Left: R.J. and Ryan in front of our
house   *Donyell McCullough*

R.J. and Holly sitting at the piano
during one of his lessons. R.J. is a
natural on the piano.
Christa Renee/AUGUST

My father, Willie Peete, and R.J., 2006   *Holly Robinson Peete*

Brother Sister Love! Ryan and R.J., summer 2009
Chris Voelker

Kwanza 2004, my last season with the Carolina Panthers
Holly Robinson Peete

Kids and Mom hanging out at the Santa Monica Pier   *Christa Renee*

Peete family at the Autism Speaks "Walk Now," LA, 2008   *Autism Speaks*

Kwanza in LA, this time with Roman   *Chris Voelker*

R.J., wide receiver for the Bears   *Peete Family*

Me, R.J., Roman, and Robinson celebrate the Pittsburgh Penguins winning the Stanley Cup, 2009. (Our friend co-owns the team.)   *Dolores Robinson*

R.J. enjoying the beach in Cabo *Holly Robinson Peete*

Left and Above: R.J. the model! Bc how times have changed. *Donyell McCullough (above), Chris Voelker (lef*

Within two weeks, Kenny carved out a little piece of time and R.J. and Holly went into the studio to record this song. Holly knocked out the main vocal, but it was too much for R.J. The mesmerizing buttons and levers in the studio, coupled with his anxiety about performing, caused him to freeze up. He wanted to play around with the equipment rather than work, and we needed to lay down a usable track.

Holly was nervous, and she wanted R.J. to be his musical self. When she started getting impatient with him, Kenny, a father himself, said they could come back another night and get it done. He gave them a file of what they had recorded so that R.J. could load it into his iPod.

R.J. listened to that piece all week long, so he could memorize his part. After he learned the whole verse and the bridge, he and Holly sang it together around the house. Watching them filled my heart. They were in such harmony, and I could see R.J. was feeling the meaning of those words.

The next time they came into the studio, he knew his part and he wasn't distracted. Kenny let him sing it through Auto-Tune, the effect fuzzing his voice and giving it a high, metallic pitch, so that he sounded like a robot singing. That was a great touch for the song and also for R.J., who now sounded like a very cool rapper. Seriously, how cool is that? Laying down a track like that in front of Babyface Edmonds. He even started calling himself R-Pain, in the style of T-Pain.

I was very excited the first time I heard that R.J. would be a part of this duet project. I had seen Wyatt and Jack Black per-

117

form their song together, and I thought this would be perfect for R.J. The song Holly wrote is so beautiful, and she did an amazing job of capturing R.J.'s voice and all of the internal struggles he has been going through.

I was driving in the car the first time I heard them sing it. Holly had left the CD in. I couldn't stop crying because the words captured the years of frustration R.J. had lived through. He was just a little kid trapped in a world he desperately wanted to get out of, but didn't know how. I am so proud of him because now he knows exactly who he is and lives with no limitations.

I often think about all the days and nights we've spent working together trying to get him to understand the most basic problems. My heart hurts for him because sometimes he just couldn't get it no matter how hard or how long we tried. But he's always had a burning desire to defeat whatever was standing in his way, and his journey has inspired me more than I have ever been inspired.

PART TWO

Advice

8

MARRIAGE

You've Got to Get
the Man Right

During the football season, most teams begin each morning with a series of meetings, hours of them, during which the coaches show the players tapes of that week's opponent so that they can assess how to take advantage of their weaknesses and maneuver past their strengths. When I played for the Detroit Lions, the first meeting of each day was with special teams coach Frank Ganz, a master motivator who knew how to get us ready to play.

Frank had a colorful history that included time spent as a marine colonel. When I worked with him, he was into his sixties, but he looked as if he was no more than forty-five. He was still trim and walked with a quick, stiff military gait. So, while we sprawled over our chairs at eight in the morning, he'd start us right off in the middle of battle.

"We landed in bad weather on Guadalcanal, so the enemy wasn't sure where we were and how many of us were there," he'd say, pacing back and forth in front of the room. "We only had one shot—one shot!—to take that position. The commanding officer said to me, and the three riflemen next to me, it was do or die, baby. One shot is all you've got. If you're not trained, not focused, not alert, you're dead. One shot. You have to be ready. You've got to get the man right."

You've got to get the man right. That was a sentence that he burned into our minds. Life is a battle, he was saying, and you don't get that many shots at success. When you go into a situation where there's a lot on the line, you've got to make sure that you're right in mind, body, and soul. Or, as he would say in another of his memorable commands, "Details, details, details. Painstaking attention to details."

He said the same thing in the locker room after practice, trying to get us to think that way when we were on our own, during our daily routines. Getting the man right is not one big decision, but a series of little decisions about everything you do during the day to keep the focus on maintaining a mind that is clear and a body that is fit. At practice, Frank stalked the sidelines screaming that phrase out through one of those old-school megaphones. Before every game, he would pace the locker room saying, "Get the man right!"

When fighting for your child, you have to be in your best shape, both mentally and physically. That's the only way you'll be able to face all the battles ahead of you. Accepting what our family was up against included realizing that we were in a fight for which I needed to get the man right. In that fight, the enemy was my child's condition, not my wife. I started out by doubting her, second-guessing her, and undermining her. When it all broke down and I was stripped of the illusions that my denial had given me, I knew the only way we could fight for our son was side by side. To do that, I wanted and needed a deeper connection to Holly. She and I had to form our own special team because beating this thing would take everything we had. At the moment my denial broke, I wasn't sure if she really trusted me. I knew, like Coach Frank said, I had to get the man right.

When people have kids, the children instantly become the most important part of their lives. Parents want to do everything for them, especially when they are babies. If a child becomes gravely ill or has a medical condition, you fight for him. But it becomes a problem when the child becomes the *only* important thing in the family. The national divorce rate hovers around 50 percent, but by some estimates, 80 percent of marriages where the couple has an autistic child come to an end. Mine almost did. Now I understand how that happened to me, and I want to give you some suggestions about what you can do so that you don't need to struggle the way that Holly and I did. It's important to remember that your behavior and attitude are the only part about this whole situation that you can control. That's where your attention must be—on the painstaking attention to the details, details, details of the relationships in your family.

I'm going to start this discussion by frankly describing what happened between Holly and me after R.J.'s diagnosis. In my talks with hundreds of families dealing with autism over the years, I've found that the troubles these marriages go through follow a pattern very similar to what we experienced.

So many marriages begin to fall apart in the wake of the grief parents feel when they get the diagnosis. When we found out R.J. had autism, it felt like losing a child. We had had years to dream the dreams that all parents have for their children, and then that child was snatched away. Sure, R.J. was still R.J., but he could no longer reciprocate our love or respond to our voices. For a good long while, there wasn't anything to replace that hope.

Holly and I both went into denial, but it took a different form for each of us. In my grief, I became defensive, refusing to accept what was right in front of my eyes. Holly went into full-on attack mode—crisis management—frantically gathering information and making contacts. This flurry of busy-ness allowed her to ignore her sorrow and her rage, putting those in a little compartment to be dealt with later.

I felt as if she had placed me in that little compartment too. I wasn't getting the attention I used to get at a time when, in reality, I needed even more. During football season, after a long day of practice, I'd call home. When we spoke, the only things she wanted to talk about were her new ideas for therapies and the latest advice she'd picked up from a book, a doctor, or another mom. Every day she had a new piece of jargon related to R.J.'s condition. At first, I'd ask her what the words meant, and to explain the abbreviations she used for different techniques or terminology. But after a while, it all started to sound like gibberish. *Okay, fine, whatever.* I didn't believe the diagnosis anyway.

The more we held our opposing positions, the wider the gap grew between us. I was shut down, withdrawn, frozen. Holly was just putting one foot in front of the other. She says now that whenever I was resistant or was unresponsive to a new therapy, she felt the clock ticking. Holly believed we were already far behind where we should have been because we got R.J. diagnosed late. If we didn't act decisively right away, we'd lose him for good. She felt that the time she spent trying to bring me up to speed was time she could have been spending on something else. Within this dwindling window of time, she didn't feel her energy was best spent coddling me.

I wasn't seeing Holly clearly either. In dismissing all the things she was trying for R.J., I dismissed her too. I was so focused on my own loneliness, that I couldn't see hers. Both of us had our moments of *Why me? Why does everyone else's kid get to be normal and mine is not? Every one of our friends' children is perfect. Our child cannot even look us in the eye.* She felt as though she had no one to talk to, no friend whose shoulder she could cry on.

When we started to heal our relationship, she described to me how during that time, she'd sometimes drop R.J. off at one of his therapies and just sit in the car and cry, "Someone has got to help me. I cannot do this all by myself." Then she'd dry her tears and go about her day. Other days, she searched the movie listings for comedies to go to, to get her mind off all of it while R.J.

was at school. Yes, she has a great group of girlfriends, but she didn't share this with them. Most of them scattered when the subject came up. The few that she did reach out to weren't much help to her. They didn't know much about autism, and it seemed to frighten them. She had made some acquaintances among the other moms of children with autism, but what she really needed was her husband, and where was he?

Suddenly after years of enjoying a deep, loving relationship that was so easy and so close, we had lost the rhythm between us. I'm a quarterback, not just on the field, but in the way I look at things. I need plays and direction. I need everything to be structured and mapped out. I hate not being fully informed and not knowing the overall plan to achieve a specific goal. On the other hand, Holly was making decisions about R.J. on the fly, making it up as she went along. All I was getting was bulletins from the front lines, notifications of things that she'd already decided, along with indications about how much this was going to cost. This world of hers and R.J.'s was spinning faster and faster, and I was just standing at the sidelines watching it accelerate. When I'd tell her to slow down because I needed a chance to think, that just made her angrier.

One of the things we used to cherish before the diagnosis was getting a chance to spend time together as a family while I was away for the season. Every month or so, Holly would get a week-long break from the sitcom she was on and she'd pack up the twins and bring them to wherever my team was playing that week. Holly and the kids watched the game and we had time together each day after practice. When autism rocked our lives, these trips turned into nightmares.

Managing twins on a plane is bad enough. But after autism manifested, R.J. was incredibly tough to travel with. He hated waiting, and unless Holly timed it so that he could board the plane the moment they got to the airport, he'd start wailing and flailing at the gate. He had to have a window seat too, or he'd spend the whole flight pushing the buttons on the armrest and kicking the seats. Holly would be so salty after getting off the plane. She'd hand me the babies and curl up in the corner, exhausted.

After the intensity involved with preparing for the game, it was hard for me to shift gears into child care. And Holly could be very critical of my interactions with R.J. She had learned so many new things about his condition that she had firm ideas about what he needed and how I should help him. Ryan was needy too. She's a sensitive girl. Even at the age of three, she picked up on all the undercurrents. Our whole family situation was so confusing to her that she could get very emotional without understanding why. Those times we all spent together made clear how far apart our family had become. I told myself that we'd piece it all back together when I got home after the season was over

However, homecoming was a shock. There was a small army of therapists coming in and out of the house at all hours. On top of that, Holly had worked up a demanding schedule for R.J. that was packed with other appointments. Clinics and wacky practitioners scattered all over Los Angeles were poking at him and leading him through some pretty crazy therapies. Holly kept reminding me that she had explained all of this to me over the phone during the season, and I couldn't deny that. But I hadn't pieced all our conversations together, brick by brick, to assemble the whole picture. I felt irrelevant to the structure she'd created for him while I was gone.

Her anger at me was always just a millimeter below the surface. If I came back from taking R.J. to one of his appointments and mentioned that I didn't think this or that seemed to be working very well, she snapped, "Who are you to come in here and tell me what to do when you've been gone for six months?"

I was undermining her efforts too, and I know she sensed that. I'm embarrassed to think back on it now. We were monitoring R.J.'s diet so carefully—even sending his poop to the lab every month to be analyzed for parasites and mineral content. Yet when I was driving him around, sometimes I'd slip him candy and products that contained wheat, like Twinkies. This was the only way I knew to reward him, and I dug the fact that we had our little father-son secret. In reality, by trying to be his cool dad, I was sending him into a hyper state and making him sick.

Tension between Holly and me became evident in other ways too. Ever since we'd first gotten married, Holly and I had always made getting time alone together a priority. Even after the kids came, Holly's mom, Dolores, helped us out. She lived close by and was always eager to babysit. But after R.J.'s diagnosis, our commitment to date night slipped from once a week, to every other week, and finally to once a month. We told each other that we were just too tired. It was more than just the exhaustion, though. When you're under a lot of stress, your libido flies out the window. And this can lead the romance to slowly leave the relationship.

Anyone with a special needs kid knows how this feels. You have knock-down-drag-outs about so many things, that you end up tiptoeing around each other just when what you really need is a place to be raw, open, and real. You've lost the safe place between you. You don't have the energy to talk about the very important subjects that need to be addressed. And you can't face another brutal, futile argument. As a result, you find yourself living within a narrower and narrower piece of who you are. No intimacy can come from that, and the absence of that connection adds another stone to your heap of sorrows.

I remember that Holly and I managed to spend a weekend away in the months after the diagnosis, but our problems were always the elephant in the room. The space between us had become another territory that autism had claimed from our lives. I still loved my spouse, but she was overloaded, overwhelmed, and couldn't stand to be touched. We couldn't communicate, and sometimes she'd have a meltdown for no apparent reason. When that happened, I would retreat into the manhole. Total shutdown. The nature of our relationship became almost clinical. You drive him to OT. I'll drive him to PT. I'll meet you back here tonight and fall asleep on the couch watching TV. And we'll do it all again tomorrow.

To her credit, Holly is not the kind of woman who will just let things go. That day when she gave me the ultimatum after my embarrassing performance at Smart Start, I understood that my wife was my one and only partner in this battle for R.J. When I promised on that day to do anything she asked, I don't think that pledge had any credibility with her. I'd been acting up and acting out in so many ways that I barely had credibility with myself at that moment. And if you need to change the world around you and your relationship to it, the way you need to start is by changing yourself. Like Coach Frank said, you have to get the man right.

I started with what men don't really like to do. I apologized. I apologized more than once.

"Holly, I am so sorry. I haven't been strong enough to be the father and the husband you need me to be. I've done our son and you a disservice. I can't tell you how helpless I feel. I want to be like you. I want to get in there and be proactive. I just feel like a burden," I said.

Holly came to my side and hugged me. "You're not a burden. I really need you."

I hugged her deeply, genuinely, for the first time in a very long while.

"I apologize and I am fully on board. Right now," I said.

All of our defenses were down. We both were crying.

"One day, when it all works out, we're going to go, 'Wow!' And we'll be so much stronger," she said.

She was right; we are so much stronger now. But to get there, I had to crash, almost like an alcoholic does when he hits rock bottom. Once I got to a place where things couldn't get any worse, all of the defenses and justifications that I'd walled myself off with were stripped away. When this happened to me, I was able to re-evaluate my actions and conceive of a different future. I no longer had to protect my way of thinking. I was open to the possibility of new ideas and interested in hearing opinions that might differ from mine. When I look back to the earlier time, I sometimes wonder what Holly must have been thinking when she saw all the things I was trying to do with R.J., and knew without a doubt that they were all wrong.

Every marriage is different. Holly's and my story may not be anything like the situation you face in your home, but since we went public with our family's story, we've found that we seem to share the broad strokes with many other families: the mom on a mission; the dad isolated and immersed in work; and the resulting strain on the marriage. While our stories are often similar, the solutions people adopt differ with every couple.

Coping with autism requires *everyone* to be on the same page. Thank God I was able to come to grips with what I needed to do and understand what Holly needed from me and—most importantly—what R.J. needed from me. Being together in the fight mends a lot of wounds.

The first thing we did was to go into counseling to address the problem. Having a safe place, with a referee to help us sort out what we had been thinking and feeling was vital to getting us facing in the same direction again. As we started that, I decided that I wanted to be involved in everything. I got to know R.J.'s therapists and started reading some of the books Holly had been handing to me. There was quite a stack of them heaped by the side of the bed, so I really went to school on this.

For some couples, this would not be a solution. Erik Linthorst, whose work with his son Graham is the subject of his film *Autistic-Like: Graham's Story,* recommends that women "give the man something he can master, some problem he can chew on and solve." Erik recalls that "we were fully engaged, but we had separate duties. I was the engine driving the research. My wife Jenny was the logistics person shuttling Graham to his appointments and assessments. The last thing she wanted to do was spend time researching chelation therapy on the Internet. We'd reconnect at the end of the day with a glass of wine and bring each other up to speed."

While that didn't work for me, it fits in with the idea of getting the man right. Erik wanted a defined problem where he could use his best skills to bring all the pieces together. This was the same situation for Chris and Tara Brancato when they took the first steps in getting treatment for their son, Luca. "I said to the shrink that I had no ability to sit there for an hour and a half and try to get him to put a block in a box," Chris said. "When the therapist said that wasn't my job, that was for a behavioral therapist, that really took a load off me. I'm really good at fighting for his rights. If the state can provide something for Luca, I'm going to make sure that he will get it."

Many men I spoke to were similar to me in that they handled their anger in an unhealthy way. Drinking too much is at the top of the list, but it includes a whole catalog of the ways that men traditionally isolate themselves. I have a lot of pain from football injuries, and the nightly scotch or two, or on other nights a pain-killer, soothed me in a way, but also ended up creating more distance between Holly and me. After we pledged to come together, I knew that habit had to go.

Once you and your spouse are on the same page with how to treat your child, the next issue that tends to come up is how to pay for it. Money can be the source of conflict in any marriage, but the cost of caring for a child with autism is staggering. For Manuel Munguia, who has three children with his wife, Deanna, the solution to Little Manny's diagnosis upended the power structure in the family. Even with both of them working, they still couldn't afford all the services that Little Manny needed. Since Deanna made more money at her job, they decided that Manuel would stay home and be the caregiver there for a few years while Deanna became the family breadwinner.

"This was a culture shift for us and for our whole family," Manuel said. "My father's position was that a man should be in the workplace and the woman should be at home. This diagnosis was a wake-up call. After we did the numbers, how could we make decisions that were only to feed my manly pride?"

The couple also asked the extended family for financial help to fill in the gap in income they would face with Manuel staying home. Everyone predicted disaster, but Manuel says the opposite came to pass. His relationship with Deanna now is stronger than ever. She sees how good Manuel is with Little Manny and how much progress her son has made with his dad around. Manuel respects his wife's judgment and instincts, as well as her hard work to support the family. "My wife and my relationship connected even more," he said. "We devoted full attention to our kids, but we never lost touch with each other. The results, you can see them. The kids are a reflection of us, of that love,"

Seems laudable when someone says that, but how do you do it? "My wife is a date-night Nazi," Erik said. "If you dare schedule anything on that night, you are going to lose a digit. Thank God she kept this through thick and thin. We get dressed up and go to a nice restaurant. I say this to other men and they snarl that it would be nice if we had the time. I always respond that you have to take the time. Your marriage is that important to you and to your child."

TIPS ON HOW TO GET THE MAN RIGHT

• GET COUNSELING: It is liberating to let your feelings out in front of a third party who will not judge you for your feelings or actions. We all must first be honest with ourselves, before we can be honest with anyone else. The sooner we men realize that we don't have all the answers, the better off we will be. Men frequently say they don't have the money for counseling, but it's a lot cheaper than divorce.

• TAKE A HARD LOOK AT YOUR DRINKING: Is it isolating you from your wife? Making your grumpy? Groggy? You need all your brain cells and every ounce of your energy for this fight. Make sure this habit isn't sapping those and building a wall between you and your wife.

• APOLOGIZE: I don't understand why men can't see how far a simple "I'm sorry" goes in mending ill will or smoothing over a mistake. And be specific with your apology. "Honey, I'm sorry for not being on board with you. You have studied and educated yourself more than me, and I wasn't there for you and our son. Please forgive me, I am ready to do *whatever* it takes."

• SHOW GRATITUDE: Everyone wants and needs to feel appreciated. I'm still learning. Men need to understand that it doesn't have to be a big elaborate party or a gift like diamonds (even though that is nice too). Simple works. Cook dinner one night or make all the plans for a spa day and romantic restaurant. Sometimes a nice foot rub is all she wants. A simple text message a few times a week that says I love you or that you're thinking about her is just as important to her as some big production that only happens once a year.

• FIGHT FAIR: Keep the fight specific. Stick to the subject you started discussing. Arguments rarely start over something personal, but they can go in that direction quickly, and then the situation deteriorates without the problem getting solved. Confine yourself to events within the last thirty-six hours. Stuff that happened six months ago is not allowed. And if either of you says,

"That means you don't love your child!" or "That means you don't really love me!"—game over. Pick it back up another time, when heads are cooler.

• GET CLEAR ABOUT THE MONEY: This is vital to keeping harmony in your marriage. In most families, one person handles the money and the other goes along with it. But this journey you're on now is an especially costly one. A couple has to decide which therapies to fund, make a budget, and raise the money from family if they can. You may need to see a financial counselor to help you structure this agreement. When you've make it, stick to it. No excuses, no slips.

• REACH OUT TO OTHER DADS: You can't just gut this out saying, *I'm fine. I'm fine.* You need other men who understand what you are going through, whether it's a father figure you can trust for good advice when the crap hits the fan, or someone from church—find that guy. As much as you love and support your wife and she does the same for you, there are parts of this that you'll feel most comfortable speaking to another guy about.

9

SIBLINGS

Little Brothers and Big Sisters

Little brothers just won't leave their big brothers alone. I should know. I was a real pest to my big brother when we were kids, and that's how we hoped that R.J.'s siblings would attach themselves to him. In fact, one of the first things we advise parents of recently diagnosed children is to have more children. A child on the spectrum can learn so much through contact with little brothers and sisters, while the child's siblings in turn learn compassion, empathy, and patience.

When Holly and I decided that we wanted to enlarge our family, our inspiration was my relationship with my brother, Skip, my childhood mentor. At three years older than me, he was always doing all the things I wanted to do, and doing them better than I could. I wanted to please him, and to impress him and his friends. I watched him carefully for clues about how I should behave if I wanted to be as cool as he was. The best thing that happened to me was that he let me tag along with him. I was lucky that he wasn't one of those brothers who said, *Oh, go away. You're the younger kid. I don't want you around.*

He played all the sports: football, basketball, and baseball. When he went to the park to play basketball or played football in the street, I was always right at his heel. I enjoyed his friends and they didn't mind having me around. This gave me a chance to play with older kids, who were stronger and more agile than my friends. This practice made me a better player against kids my own age.

I always wanted to go into my brother's room and play with his much cooler stuff. I was so jealous when he started taking drum lessons. Our parents said I'd have to wait until I was as old as Skip to play drums. Whenever I knew he'd be late in getting back from school or from practice, I'd sneak into his room and attack those drums. As much as I tried to hide the evidence that I'd been there, he always seemed to know.

After we got R.J. on to the right track with his therapies, I thought back to the way I used to pester my brother and try to provoke a reaction from him. This was basically the same thing that we were paying therapists thousands of dollars a month to do with R.J.—keeping him constantly engaged, constantly drawing him back to the complications of the world. When the dust settled, and we felt as though we'd set up a pretty good system for R.J., we decided that we wanted to have more children. Mainly it was because we loved raising our twins, but we also expected that one of the side benefits would be that his younger siblings would always be all up in R.J.'s business.

As I'm writing this now, I think that is one of the smartest decisions Holly and I made. Robinson and Roman are great kids, and we can't imagine our family life without them. Plus having two pesky little brothers, our two little accidental therapists, has taken a lot of pressure off Ryan.

When R.J. withdrew, it was extremely traumatic for Ryan. They had been buddies who did everything together and communicated in unique ways that they had invented. To Holly and me, it seemed like a lot of baby gibberish, but the way they looked at each other and responded when they were babbling made us certain that they were talking in their own way. Then all of a sudden, R.J. was in the corner, unresponsive, and that connection was lost. I watched Ryan try to engage him without any success. She would try to roll a ball back and forth with him, but he would just sit in the corner spinning the wheels on one of his toy cars. Ryan had suddenly lost her buddy, and it was confusing for her. We could see that she was sad, but she was too young to express how she felt.

She realized that there was something going on with him even before Holly and I were wise to it, and she became his guardian angel, always looking out for him. If we yelled upstairs that it was time to eat, she would make sure, wherever he was, and whatever he was doing, that he knew that we were expecting him and that he put down what he was doing and came with her. She would even grab him by the hand and make sure he came with her.

Twins are usually strongly bonded, but Ryan's personality

compelled her to take responsibility for R.J. She's always been big-hearted, almost to a fault. She wants harmony in every minute of her life, and she craves everyone getting along. It can be overwhelming for her when someone throws a monkey wrench into a comfortable situation. Our concern was that her strong feelings of protective responsibility would prevent her from living her own life because she believed it was her duty to look out for her R.J.

We could see she was always thinking, *Is he okay? Is this going to be too much for him?* In the years before we understood how to handle social situations with R.J., events like birthday parties would make Holly and me extremely anxious on the twins' behalf. Video recordings of probably every birthday we attended for the first five years of their lives contain the background soundtrack of R.J. having a meltdown. We'd be on constant alert to decide the moment when we had to make a hasty good-bye so as not to ruin everybody else's fun. Even then, when Ryan was just in preschool, she wasn't embarrassed that her brother had acted out and she didn't sulk because she had to leave. Her concerns were always for her brother and how hard this was for him. She used to get very upset that she didn't know how to soothe him—an early sign that she identified more with his pain and discomfort than she did with her own.

In enrolling R.J. in the Lab School, the goal always was to get him into an elementary school with typical children so he could benefit from the challenges that would arise from that contact. Ryan liked the Lab School, but she'd been sad that she wasn't with her brother. The day we told Ryan that she and R.J. would be together in school again was a very happy day.

One week a few months after R.J.'s arrival at Ryan's school, Ryan seemed a little under the weather. Holly asked her if she wanted to stay home from school, but she insisted that she was fine and she wanted to go. At school, she was listless, and when the school nurse was notified, it was determined that she was running a fever. When Holly went to bring her home, Ryan started crying in the car that she didn't want to leave R.J. alone. "No one will be there to protect him," she sobbed. "When the other kids say mean things about him, I tell them they're wrong. If he could talk, he'd tell them what a good kid he is."

We realized then how much Ryan had taken on and how unfair it was to burden her like that. When the kids at school made fun of R.J., it hurt her too. She was too loyal to side with the kids against R.J., even though that would have made things easier for her socially. In assuming the role of his protector, she wasn't able to address her own difficulties with fitting in.

In a way, it was inevitable that Ryan would get less attention than R.J. We felt terrible about it, but you can understand how this sometimes happens in the families of children with special needs. Those families have a line item list for the special needs child that is four or five times greater than the one for their unaffected siblings. So much of their energy has to go there, that the parents are just relieved that the other children aren't too much trouble. But if you keep your focus oriented that way, you'll miss the fact that your other children have needs too.

We made it a mission to make sure that Ryan wasn't neglected. We decided that our first step was to bring Ryan into the discussion of what was going on with R.J. Of course, she knew on a day-to-day basis what his difficulties were—probably better than we did. But we wanted her to understand the reason behind R.J.'s problems. We thought that giving her words to describe what she saw and felt about his differences could help her better handle this situation.

Holly and I thought it over for a long time before we had this talk with Ryan. We wanted to get it right, to find a balance between giving her enough information so that she had a better understanding of him, and not overwhelming her with medical jargon and details. We thought that the most important element to the discussion was to make it safe for her to express what she had been feeling. We also wanted to give her hope by pointing out how much R.J. was improving. We didn't want to do to Ryan what had been done to us when we first found out about R.J.'s condition. Besides, there was a lot to be hopeful about. R.J. was already making incredible progress.

When we sat her down for this talk, R.J. was working with one of his therapists outside the room, so that we could all speak freely and express whatever emotions we felt at that moment. I know all of us were a little nervous. Holly and I had never tried explaining this before. We'd only talked in a general way about it to adults, and the questions they asked about autism were logical and practical, mostly about R.J.'s chances and his future. We weren't sure what kinds of questions Ryan would ask us.

I think when any kid is asked to sit down for a talk with Mom and Dad, he or she assumes something is wrong. Ryan was squirming in her seat, her hands clenched at her sides. You could see the relief spread through her body when she found out this was about R.J.

"Ryan, you know, your brother doesn't get things as quickly as you do," I started off. "It takes a little more time for his mind to come into focus."

"I know," she said.

"Sometimes when you want to play with him, he doesn't look up at you," Holly continued. "And when you speak to him, he doesn't answer back."

"It's because his brain doesn't work the same way yours does," I said. "He's got something that the doctors call autism."

"Autism," Ryan repeated. "Autism? I thought people called him 'artistic.' I thought they thought he was good at art."

We laughed, but we returned to giving her a better sense of what autism meant. As we described it to her in the most basic terms, it seemed as if a little bit of the weight of this had already lifted from her, because she finally had a name for it.

"You know all the special teachers that come to the house to work with R.J.?" Holly asked.

"Yes, but they don't teach him things. They just play," Ryan said. Can't fool this child about anything.

"That's school for him," Holly continued. "All the things that you do, that other kids do, just naturally, he has to be taught how to do. You know, like we have to teach him to look up at us when we call his name. And we have to show him how when you throw him a ball, you want him to throw it back. All those things are part of the different way his mind works. The best way to teach him these things is to have fun with him. It might look like play to you, but in every one of those sessions, he is learning."

Suddenly we could see the lightbulb going on in Ryan's head.

"You have to teach him how to be a kid," she said.

"Exactly!" I said.

Ryan started to cry, but this time it was tears of relief.

"Ryan, don't cry," Holly said. "You know that R.J. is getting better every day and that all this work he's doing is helping him a lot."

"Sometimes I feel like I don't have a twin brother," she said. "I see other twins together, and it's not that way with R.J."

Holly and I looked at each other in shock. We hadn't had any idea how hard this was on Ryan: the strong, sweet girl who always seemed completely on top of every social situation, the girl who was always at ease in her school and within the family. She hadn't shown us any of her sorrow and loneliness. Or worse: maybe she had, and we were so consumed with managing R.J., that we hadn't noticed.

"Oh, honey, you and R.J. are close," Holly said. "It's just that he can't express it as well as other kids."

"Maybe those people need to teach me how to play with R.J.," Ryan said.

The experts say that when a family has a special needs child, all the other members of the family also have special needs. We all needed to learn how to communicate with R.J. through play, but only Holly and I had had the lessons. The next day, we set up sessions where Ryan could learn how to understand what pleased R.J. and find a way to join in that was fun for both of them. We also understood something else: Ryan needed her own special time.

We had been so concerned about bringing R.J. up to speed, all the while spending so much money and time, that we couldn't see how neglected Ryan felt. She was too young to express it, but we believed that if we let it go on for much longer, then Ryan would start to have her own issues. There always had been mother/daughter shopping trips and confidences, but we needed to bring that up a notch. Holly decided she needed to commit to taking Ryan out to dinner alone once a month.

As much as Ryan claimed she didn't feel that special twin connection to R.J., she still saw herself as his guardian. When kids are first at elementary school, the boys pretty much stay with the boys, and the girls play with the girls. Ryan could be all the way on the other side of the yard playing tetherball, but she'd know when R.J. skinned his knee. She'd go running over to see if he needed to go to the nurse's office, as if she was his mom. Part of this was just the kind of person she is. She very well might have done the same if she was the eldest child and none of her siblings had autism. But R.J. did have autism, and the obligation she felt to make sure he was physically, emotionally, and socially okay was something we wanted to spread around a little bit more by having more children.

Robinson was born when R.J. and Ryan were six. R.J. had come a long way in the two years since we started aggressively treating his autism. He was responding to us more consistently and he could tell us when he wanted to eat or when he needed something. He was integrated into a regular school with Ryan and he had a few friends. Robinson came along at just the right time.

R.J. adored him right from the start. Robinson was his little toy, and he didn't want to go anywhere without him. He could look at Robinson for hours at time. He even wanted to sleep in the same bed as his little brother. We thought part of what attracted R.J. to Robinson was the fact that Robinson, like R.J., didn't really know how to use his words. They developed their own nonverbal communication. Also, parents can get tired of playing a game with a baby, who seems to have an endless tolerance for repetition. Luckily for Robinson and for R.J., they both could do the same thing for hours on end. R.J. liked nothing better than getting a laugh out of Robinson, who was pretty easy to get laughing. All of this seemed like the most brilliant idea. Robinson was a great addition to the family. We all loved him and he was great for R.J.

Yes, it was all great, until Robinson started to talk.

Somewhere between the ages of two and three, it was clear that Robinson was very advanced in his ability to communicate. He learned to talk, and he hasn't stopped since. Through that, Robinson made that journey that all little brothers make, from being fascinating to being annoying. All little brothers look up to their big brothers, just as I had. I think the first full sentence out of Robinson's mouth to R.J. was "Play with me."

Robinson is such an outgoing personality that he's always all up under R.J. He never lets him retreat. You never know what is going to come out of Robinson's mouth. Being able to react to the unknown is a big part of what R.J. needs preparation for before he gets out into a world where things come at you from many different directions. When R.J. turned Robinson down for a game of catch, he had to say more than a simple "No." Robinson wouldn't accept that short of an answer. He'd just keep at him. If you are going to live in the same house with each other, you've got figure out how to make that work.

As Robinson grew, his natural talents were obvious. He, like R.J., was a gifted athlete. The first time Robinson held a bat, he held it the right way. When he runs, he's got naturally good form. By the time Robinson turned three, there were some things that he was better at than R.J. When R.J. was nine, we saw he was starting to resent Robinson, whose vocabulary was by then off the charts. R.J. didn't want to play with Robinson because he didn't want his little brother to show him up.

R.J. has a fascination with basketball, and he's got a spectacular memory. He knows just about every player in the NBA, and he follows the trades and reads on the Internet about all the games. He's often a source of news for me about what's going on in basketball. One day, he blew me away by identifying a minor player we saw walking down the street in LA, a guy who wasn't even wearing his uniform. Basketball is R.J.'s thing, and I'm proud of him for how much he studies and retains.

Last year R.J., Robinson, and I were watching the NBA finals, and Robinson for the first time got caught up in the excitement. He started asking me questions about the game, and I was explaining some of the rules and the strategy behind the plays. I could see R.J. moving around on the couch, getting a little jumpy as his little brother soaked up new information. Robinson asked me to identify some of the players. I pointed our Derek Fisher, who had just made a spectacular three-point shot. "That's Pau Gasol and over there is Sasha Vujacic."

"Don't tell him everything," R.J. blurted out. "Don't tell him everything. That's mine."

For a moment I was shocked. I wanted to correct R.J. He shouldn't be restricting his brother.

"Teach him hockey. Teach him something else," R.J. said. "Basketball is mine."

Then it hit me, as it continues to hit me day in and day out with R.J. He was having a normal sibling response, which is much more than we were ever led to think he'd be capable of. He didn't want that little pest of a brother inching in on his territory, which was understandable for any brother, but particularly R.J., for whom everything had been so hard won.

This is exactly what we'd hoped would happen when we had more children, but we couldn't have predicted how perfectly the personalities of his twin sister and his little brother would work in tandem to keep R.J. growing and changing. His sister is his protector. They are in the same classes at school. She makes sure he's got his homework done because she's compulsive about completing her own assignments. She's always asking him if he's been marking off pages for the reading diary they've been assigned.

If Ryan is his guardian angel, Robinson is his Energizer Bunny, who forces him to respond. Sometimes we'll hear R.J. saying, "Robinson, please leave me alone. Robinson! Get out of here!" I have to stop myself from going in there and saying, *R.J., we don't want you yelling at your brother like that.* Robinson's forcing a spontaneous reaction out of R.J., and that's a good thing. R.J. is successfully communicating to Robinson that he cannot slip into R.J.'s world as much as he'd like.

As school was winding down last year, Ryan was the one who was having social problems, as many girls do when they hit that preteen stage. Some girls who had been her friends for as long as she'd been in school had stopped including her. They no longer invited her over to their houses. You know the mean girl phase, where some girls decide they are the coolest and other girls who don't wear the right jeans, or know the latest band, or don't shun the girls the "cool" girls have decided need to be shunned, are also kicked out of the club. Ryan was confused. She'd talked to her mom about it, but Mom's advice hadn't helped her as much as she needed.

I was in the kitchen getting myself a snack while R.J. and Ryan were sitting at the kitchen table working on their homework. The homework wasn't getting much attention as Ryan described the latest slight. She'd been invited to a cool girl's birthday party and wanted to bring along another girl, someone who had been included in the group for the last four years but had recently fallen out of favor. The hostess let her know that this was un-cool. Ryan was torn up. She wanted to go to the party, but she didn't want to be disloyal to her other friend.

I watched as she described the elaborate politics of fifth-grade friendship, but I confess, my eyes were trained on R.J. He'd put his pencil down, his hands flat on the table as he looked directly at Ryan while she told her tale. I could see strong emotions on his face. He loves his sister, and he hated to see her go through stuff like this. R.J. knows all of those girls too, and I'm sure he's got his feelings about how they've treated him.

"Ryan, why are you friends with that girl?" he asked. "She's mean to you, so don't be her friend. You've got to stand up for yourself."

"These are my friends!" Ryan protested, on the verge of tears. "They've been my friends since kindergarten. We were all friends and I just want everyone to get along and to be happy."

"Ryan, why are you friends with that girl?" R.J. asked. "She's mean to you, so don't be her friend."

I might have thought that R.J. was having an inappropriate response. He just kept repeating himself, like one of his old stimming habits, but in a more complex form. But the truth was that Ryan wasn't answering the question he was asking, so it made sense that he would ask it again. In fact, he asked it a third time, and he still didn't get what I would consider a proper response from his sister. There was much more going on at that table than R.J. demanding that his sister answer his question.

I don't think Holly and I in our determination to fight back against autism could have ever imagined the scene I saw at the kitchen table that night: R.J. giving his sister social and emotional guidance. Here was a boy who eight years earlier didn't appear to have any emotional connections, who couldn't express himself or respond to the emotions of others. Now here he was having the kind of communication that a lot of preteen boys have trouble with even if they aren't on the spectrum. This was extraordinary no matter who the brother and sister were.

There were hundreds of things we tried in our campaign to ensure that R.J. would have as close to a normal childhood as we could create. The therapies, the diet, sports, music, and carefully selected video games all played a part in his growth. I don't think any of those things were as important as R.J. having three siblings who love him, watch out for him, and just plain won't leave him alone. He's part of a family, and his participation in it matters to everyone around him.

As I was standing there in the kitchen watching R.J. and Ryan with my heart swelling in paternal pride, Robinson came in all animated, motor mouth. "What are you guys doing? Can I sit with you? Do you want to get a snack? Dad, can we go out and get ice cream?"

"Robinson, get out of here. We've got to do our homework!" R.J. said.

"Hey, R.J., do you want to play Madden Football? I bet I can beat you this time. If I say so myself, I think I'm getting pretty good at it. In fact . . ."

"Robinson, leave me alone! Dad, Robinson's bothering me. Can you make him go away?"

No, I thought. *I'm happy to say, R.J., that's something you're going to have to sort out yourself.*

TIPS ON SIBLINGS

• HAVE MORE CHILDREN! I'm sure some of you will groan at the idea of another child in the house, but I'm convinced, as I've laid out in this chapter, that our family is better off and R.J. is a more self-sufficient and compassionate person because his siblings have encouraged him along and protected him when he's had troubles. Think carefully about this, though. If you have a child with autism, there is an increased chance your next child will have it too. Holly and I believed strongly that a cluster of vaccines kicked off R.J.'s autism. As a result, we were very careful in spacing out when Robinson and Roman got their vaccinations.

• TELL THE SIBLINGS ABOUT AUTISM: The other kids need to know why their sibling with autism sometimes doesn't look them in the eye or answer them when they call. You have to make sure when you talk to the siblings, that the information you're giving them is appropriate for their age level, not too full of jargon and medical terms. This is a subject that should be revisited from time to time because the brothers and sisters can take in more technical information about it as they get older.

• MAKE SPECIAL TIME FOR THE OTHER KIDS: So much of the family's energy goes to the child with special needs, that the other children can feel neglected. Holly has tried to compensate for this by taking Ryan on trips to New York where they got to spend some one-on-one time together. I've also taken Ryan out for nights alone with Dad. Let the child pick the place and allow him or her to decide what you'll talk about. If you guide the conversation, you may end up talking about the special needs child, which is a mistake—each child needs a moment to shine. Discipline yourself to talk about the child who is sitting in front of you. Ask questions about that child's interests. This is your chance to get to know the child a little better and make sure that he or she feels well loved.

• DON'T MAKE THE SIBLINGS MINI ADULTS: Some kids with active, empathetic minds, like Ryan, take on adult concerns too easily. They worry about the sibling's future and social life. If you think your child is taking on more than he or she should, talk to the child about how this is really the parents' responsibility and get the child to see a counselor if you think that will help.

• HELP THE SIBLINGS HANDLE GUILT: Some siblings feel guilty that their brother or sister has such a tough time with basic life tasks they find so easy. Some parents tell their kids, "Stop whining and consider yourself lucky." That's not very helpful. Siblings need to grieve, as Ryan did, for the loss of a sibling who could communicate intuitively with them. We all want our children to be compassionate, but you don't want the sibling to feel he or she can't excel beyond the special needs child's capabilities.

• COMMUNICATE: Siblings need to know that they can always ask you or the doctor questions. They should know that you believe that their questions are important. Some children think that their questions will upset their parents and make them a target for any frustration or anger that the parents might feel about the situation. Only you can make it safe for them to express these feelings. Compliment your child for asking an intelligent question.

• TALK ABOUT FAMILY TROUBLES AFTER THE KIDS ARE IN BED: There is a lot of stress in any family of a child with special needs. The parents have scheduling difficulties and money woes times ten. Try to have these discussions after the children have gone to bed. Some children will feel inhibited from asking for what they need, because they don't want to burden their parents any further.

10

TOUGH LOVE

Discipline and a Special Needs Child

In summer of 2000, in East Chop on Martha's Vineyard we rented a Victorian house that was big enough for our whole extended family. This grand old seven-bedroom house stood on two acres of land and had a big back porch that overlooked the beach. I was playing for the Oakland Raiders then and kept a rigorous workout schedule during our vacation so that I could stay ready for the season.

I started every morning with a run down to the beach, along the shore, and back to the house. I was always cautious at the corner at the back of the property. At that rounded corner, with no stop sign or yield sign, traffic merged nonstop from one street into the next. The sun-blinded vacationers barely slowed down at that curve. If I ran into that street without looking, it would be all over.

The days were beautiful and relaxing. With so much family

around, the twins, who were nearly three, had plenty of people fussing over them. After my workout and lunch, I usually sat on the porch and looked out at our unobstructed view of the deep blue water. There I heard the sweet sounds of Ryan playing with her grandma, Holly chasing R.J. around in the yard, against the background sound of the gentle lapping of the waves on the shore and the traffic zooming around the corner.

One afternoon, I was in Holly's and my room getting a cigar to enjoy on the porch, where no one could complain about smell, when through the window, I heard Holly giving R.J. some mommy orders. "Get back here, R.J. Put that down." I peered out the window and saw him in the middle of the lawn ignoring his mom, as toddlers sometimes do. He kept moving farther away as Holly's voice got more commanding. "Come back! Come back! R.J.! Stop!" I turned back to get my smoke, then stopped cold.

I heard Holly leap up out of the Adirondack chair and go pounding down the steps from the porch to the yard. "R.J.! NO!" she screamed. I rushed to the window to see what was going on. R.J., only a few feet from the street, was running full tilt away from his mom, laughing. Holly was in full-on chase mode in her flip-flops, which were not letting her run as fast as she needed to go. "R.J., STOP IT! COME BACK HERE!"

I raced downstairs to the porch. Holly was a good twenty yards away from R.J. when his feet hit the asphalt of that dangerous turn. He was looking back at his mom, instead of peering ahead to see if any cars were rushing around that turn. We wouldn't know until a few months later that R.J.'s autism prevented him from reading the panic and horror on Holly's face. He thought this was one big game.

I've had my share of nightmares, but this was the scariest moment of my life. In my worst nightmares, someone is after me and I can't move. A different version of that was happening here. They were too far away for me to do anything. I stood frozen on the porch thinking, *I can't get to him. I can't get to him.* I was sure I was about to watch both of them be killed.

Holly ran out onto the street with no more fear than R.J. had shown. He was in the middle of the street at the yellow line when she grabbed him. The fact that there was no traffic at that moment was a miracle. Both of them could have been hit.

When Holly got to him, she first hugged him tightly, then kissed him on the top of the head. From all the way up on the porch I heard her say, "Don't you ever do that again!" Then right there in the middle of the street, she pulled his pants down and spanked him five times. Cars slowed down to watch. She dragged him out of the street and back up to the house.

Holly and I hardly ever spank our kids. We agreed before we had them that spanking was the punishment of last resort. I believe this was the first time either of the twins had been punished in that way. When she got back to the porch holding our sobbing little boy, the look on her face had so many shades of emotion: relief, love, frustration, embarrassment, terror, with fury just starting to fade. "It was just instinct," she said before I could even ask her a question. "I had to. I wanted him to remember what he did."

But would he?

Our summer in East Chop was the last one before we got the diagnosis. We knew that something was wrong, but we didn't yet know what. Spanking him wasn't the right approach to getting him to understand danger, we later came to understand. Still, everything that happened in that episode illustrated something about the way parents have to think when they discipline autistic and special needs children.

Parents teach their children every minute of the day. We're supposed to model good behavior with every interaction. That's why we wait with them for the light to change when we're standing at the corner to cross the street when we'd have jaywalked if we'd been on our own. Or why we say "shoot" or "fudge" when we stub our toes on the kitchen table at breakfast. Our first responsibility is to teach them to keep themselves safe. Second come the lessons on telling right from wrong. If they pick up common-sense safety lessons, good manners, and respectful behavior, that's the parental trifecta.

When we first arrived in East Chop, we'd warned both of the kids not to stray too far from the house. Ryan understood right away, and we never had to tell her again. Not so with R.J. We thought that the surprise of being spanked would have burned into R.J.'s brain the facts that there were consequences for not listening to Mom and that there was danger in the street at the edge of the lawn. At first, he seemed to get it. Yet the next day he was right over there, close enough to the edge that if he'd decided to make a break for it, we wouldn't have been able to stop him in time. This time I was in the yard too, because Holly and I recognized that we had to do a better job of monitoring him. Still, this boy needed another talking-to. I walked over to him casually and, once I was there, grabbed him by the shoulders and spoke to him in my stern dad voice.

"R.J., you cannot go this close to the street. Do you understand me?" I told him, looking him directly in the eyes. He squirmed in my arms and his gaze wandered all over the place, anywhere but toward me. "Listen to me. Listen to me. Do you understand what I'm saying? You cannot go past this bush. You do, and you're in big trouble with me and with Mom. Do you hear me?"

He had a sarcastic smile on his face that made me think that he was hearing me but refusing to listen.

"R.J., what did I just say? R.J.! What did I say?"

"No street."

"Right, and where is it you have to stop?"

"Not in the street."

"At this bush, R.J. You can't go past this bush."

"Bush."

Even though he repeated the right words, a few hours later he was back at that edge. Another talking-to did not change anything.

We decided we needed to give him a boundary.

We put up markers for him: an old bicycle, a boogie board, and some cans. We all hated the way it made the yard look, but if it would cue R.J., well, we'd just have to deal. We had to change our behavior. Every time we let R.J. play in the yard, we decided that we needed to have an adult within a few feet of him. Was it some boy thing, this attraction to danger? Whether it was due to mischief, defiance, or inattention, we just couldn't take another chance that he'd bolt. These changes did the trick. We were able to keep him out of traffic for the rest of the vacation.

The first time around, we did pretty much everything wrong in trying to keep him out of the street. We spanked him when it wasn't clear that he really knew what he was being spanked for. We lectured him when he couldn't retain that message. It's hard to remember what we were thinking back then, but I know that a part of me thought that he was just being a troublemaker. At the time, we didn't know he was on the spectrum, and we hadn't figured out how to effectively discipline a child with autism.

This would come up on our plane trip home too. R.J. was one of those kids who kicked the seat in front of him, and the plane trip back from Martha's Vineyard was no exception. We got settled in our seats, and he started kicking, wiggling against the seat belt, and pressing the flight attendant call button over and over. I looked at him firmly and told him to stop. He didn't pay any attention to me. He didn't look up at the sound of my voice. In fact, scolding him just made him kick harder and faster. This infuriated me. It was so disrespectful that he wasn't listening to his father. I grabbed his legs.

"I'm going to give you one more chance, R.J." I said. "You know you're not supposed to kick the seat. You have one more chance or I'm not going to give you the snack Mommy packed for you."

Raising my voice or threatening him with consequences had no impact. Meanwhile the other passengers on the plane were giving me the kinds of looks people give you when you can't control your children. I didn't know then that it wasn't that he was being disobedient or disrespectful. I wouldn't understand until the next summer that the real problem was that R.J. simply had no idea what I wanted from him.

That Martha's Vineyard trip had been an eye-opener for me as a new father. When Holly and I were first married, I'd be contemptuous when I saw parents ignoring their kids who were running wild in the grocery store, or parents trying to reason with a child who was endlessly kicking the seat on a plane. I'd tell Holly that someone needed to take that child in hand and say, "This is over right now. When we get home, there are going to be consequences." As far as I was concerned, the power in those families was all out of balance. The kids were running the parents, who seemed to be asking, rather than commanding, that their children obey.

I know you know what I'm talking about here. Some kid is pulling stuff off the shelves in the supermarket or throwing herself on the floor and staging a temper tantrum because Dad won't buy her a cookie at the bakery. I hated it when the parent would talk in a measured, gentle voice. *You know, Megan, that's not okay. Use your words. What are you really trying to express? I know you are disappointed right now because Daddy won't let you have a cookie. But sometimes we don't get what we want in life.* How is a kid supposed to understand that? And why should you have to reason with her? *I am not going to be that parent,* I used to tell Holly. *I'm the authority. I'm the parent, and your job, my child, is not to question me.*

Yet gradually I came to understand that that was exactly the kind of parent I needed to be for R.J.

Since the beginning of time, toddlers have run toward danger, laughing all the way, while their frantic parents chase after them. Once their parents get their arms around them, they want to shake the kids up in a way that will make them remember that what they did was wrong. But when your child is on the spectrum, you can't just go with this instinct, as Holly and I had. Each child on the spectrum can respond to a different approach. You need to figure out how best to communicate with your child.

When we were just beginning to learn how to handle R.J.'s autism, one of the first things we were taught was how differently kids on the spectrum take in the world. This affects the ways you can punish them. For example, since their sensory systems are all out of whack, kids with autism have a different relationship to pain. While some kids with autism can feel that a blanket sliding across their arm is as excruciating as being set on fire, a different kid will under-react to actual pain. He could be sitting next to a hill of fire ants and be bitten a hundred times without making a peep. Knowing that, we realized that a spanking could have been either a cruel overreaction or a useless nonevent.

Holly spanking R.J. was an ineffective punishment for other reasons too. She felt so guilty afterward. Many times affected children can't connect the punishment with their bad behavior, so they think you are just hitting them for no reason. Hitting them might also hurt them socially as well as physically. Many kids with autism hit and bite their peers. They can't control themselves, and they don't understand when they've hurt another person. Even kids who don't naturally express their frustrations with their fists or their teeth can pick it up from the other kids at school. And if their parents hit them to punish them, they might think it's okay to lash out at school or at their brothers and sisters. We were fortunate that R.J. never was a hitter or a biter.

We learned that when he misbehaved we needed to do exactly what those parents I'd looked down on had done with their children: we had to reason with him. We also had to watch him carefully to discover the things that motivated him, again trying to find his internal driver. *What drives R.J.? What does he want?* Once we found out, we knew that rewarding him with those things and punishing him by taking them away, would make a big impact on him, just as it does with any kid. When you uncover what can motivate your child, then you can understand how to discipline that child, though with a child on the spectrum you've still got to handle everything about this with a lot of care.

We found out early on that R.J. liked video games. As he got older, he sometimes figured out how to work his way through one without anyone teaching him. This is where his hyper-focus became useful for him. He'd fiddle with it and fiddle with it until, by trial and error, he figured out how to get Pac-Man to the next level. His cousin, who is three years older, taught him some of the tricks of Madden Football, and he was fixated on that for a while. We'd warn him when bedtime was coming up. But sometimes, even when we gave him plenty of reminders, he still wouldn't want to put down the game.

All kids can pitch a fit when you break them away from something they want to do. Ryan and our next youngest, Robinson, who is six years younger than the twins, might also cry when they don't want to go to bed. But you can say to them, "Look, these are Mom and Dad's rules. You go to bed at eight thirty. Turn this off and do as you are told. That's it." You let them cry. They'll cry themselves to sleep. But they would understand what happened.

If R.J. didn't want to go to bed and I took the controller away from him or shut off the television, I could launch him to a serious meltdown because he couldn't understand why I wanted to separate him from this moment. If I told him to go to his room, where he was isolated from everything else, his obsessive behavior might kick in, and the energy he'd devote to it would amaze us. Fixating on the fact that he wanted to play his game, he would go on crying in his room for eight hours. No parent can tolerate that, and it's a terrible thing to do to a child, no matter what your intentions are.

When he was in that mode, you couldn't reach him. "Why are you stopping me? Why? Why? I like to play video games! WHY?"

When this happened, we were faced with a dilemma. We were as firm about R.J.'s bedtime or dinnertime as we were for the other kids. He had to follow the rules, and this could sometimes lead to a meltdown. This meant that in addition to enforcing the rules, one of us would have to sit with him as he rocked, screamed, and cried. Enforcing the rules with him meant punishing us too. As he wailed, Holly or I would hold his arms and explain in that measured voice, "I know you really want to play Pac-Man, R.J., but it's time for bed. I understand you don't want to do this, but these are the rules." It really took a tremendous amount of patience to calm him down. This could go on for a half hour or more.

In order to get him to follow the rules without having a meltdown, we couldn't be as abrupt and stern with him as we were with our other children. We first had to consider what space he was in and try to join him there so we could understand the most effective way to get him to obey. We had to give him plenty of warning that we expected something from him. To make sure he heard us, we had to reinforce that warning with direct contact.

On planes, I understood it was useless to just say, "Stop it. Don't do it again." I had to touch him and get him to look at me. Once he was looking at me, I had to explain what I wanted slowly and carefully. "It's not appropriate to kick someone's seat. And if you do that, it's going to make them angry and me angry, and that's not going to feel good." Then I might have to show him what I meant by gently pounding on his back repeatedly so he understood how annoying that sensation was. Physical things like that made a big impression on him.

Once I had his attention, I would say, "How does this feel? It doesn't feel very good. That's what you're doing to the person in front of you. That's not okay. Kicking the seat is bothering that other gentleman. Do you understand that? Do you understand me?" I had to repeat it several times, until he said, "Okay, I get it." This would happen a few times a flight because after an hour, he'd forget what I'd said and start kicking. I'd have to start all over again.

We've had the experience of having a grumpy old man on the plane ask, "Why are you indulging that kid? Just make him stop kicking the seat," I wanted to say, *That doesn't work,* but I had to just bite my tongue. I can't count the number of times I've had to suppress the urge to give one of those grumpy guys a lecture. *My kid's on the spectrum. He doesn't understand that. I'm not indulging him. This is the most effective way to get him to stop. And why don't you shut up by the way?* To think I used to be that guy.

My friend Manuel Munguia has a five-year-old son, Little Manny, who's on the spectrum. He's been working hard with Little Manny's therapists to teach him how to cross the street, but after two years of lessons every day, Little Manny still can't get it.

"He knows to stop, but he doesn't look both ways," Manuel said. "I'm hard on him a hundred percent of the time because I know he only gets thirty percent of what I'm saying. I use an authoritative tone because I want him to know the tone of my voice. When he knows Daddy is upset, he says he's sorry, but he sometimes doesn't catch on as to what he is supposed to be sorry about."

Little Manny's basic safety is a huge concern for his family. It's put them in a two-year state of emergency. They're halfway there if at least Little Manny knows to stop.

Manuel is trying to use his emotion to communicate with his son, but he's also trying really hard to find Little Manny's internal drivers. A few months back, the Munguia family—mom Deanna, and kids Isabella, six, Little Manny, five, and Elizabeth, three—went to Disneyland. Manuel expected that the crowds and the noise would trigger dozens of meltdowns for Little Manny, but he and Deanna thought it was worth making the attempt for the sake of Isabella and Elizabeth, who they knew would love the vacation. They bought a VIP pass so that Little Manny wouldn't have to wait in long lines. This is a very smart move, by the way—lines drive kids on the spectrum insane, even mild-mannered ones like R.J.

Manuel said that Little Manny handled everything very well. He was so caught up in seeing the characters and the rides for small children that he didn't get overwhelmed until they were standing in the relatively short VIP line for Peter Pan. Manuel said that normally he would have insisted that Little Manny stay with the family and behave. He would have used the experience as a lesson in delayed gratification. But his understanding of Little Manny had evolved as they worked for so long on the right way to cross the street. Manuel understood how hard it was for Little Manny to understand what was expected of him. So when Little Manny started to yell outside Peter Pan, Manuel saw this as a good opportunity to spend some time with him and maybe try to better understand him. In addition, it gave Deanna and the girls a break.

"I tried to follow his direction," Manuel said. "I asked him where he wanted to go. He can't express himself verbally, so I let him take my hand and guide me. 'Where do you want to go? Do you want to go outside? Show me.' We ended up at a shaded table where we could just chill out. He just needed a little time. If you watch him, he can show you what he wants. He can help me figure out what soothes him and what kind of pace he needs to stay calm."

As difficult as it is to raise a child on the spectrum, it's good to remember that raising typical kids also has its challenges. When you have a child with autism, you always need to check yourself to see if a particular issue is a result of your child's special needs, or if your kid is just being a kid, doing what any kid would do.

"There are times when I worry that I give Luca a free pass on a lot of things," said Chris Brancato, whose six-year-old son is on the spectrum. "I wouldn't hesitate to tell his sisters to sit down and eat their cereal. But how can I expect him to sit down in a chair for a whole meal? Sometimes, I think that no other people in the world have to deal with the kinds of problems that I have with Luca. Then I talk to my friends and I find out that all of their sons also have a hard time sitting through a meal."

And just like parents of typical children, parents of special needs kids are always checking and comparing their children to others to gauge how they're progressing. But it's important to understand that every child on the spectrum improves at that child's own pace. It could be that Manuel shows Little Manny how to cross the street every day for four years without getting any sense that he's making progress, then one day he just gets it. He knows it and he has it nailed for the rest of his life. No timetables or projections are going to help you; you've just got to be ready to move forward with your child as he or she develops.

R.J. made so much progress at the ages of six, seven, and eight, that he just astonished us with how many things he could accomplish. In that time, we'd also learned how best to manage him. To avoid meltdowns, we capitalized on his love of having a clear schedule laid out for him in advance. We even bought a special timer for him so he could watch the minutes ticking off. We had to remind him half an hour before bed that he had thirty minutes to go. Then we'd remind him at fifteen, ten, and five minutes. Now he can do that himself by setting the timer on his cell phone.

In fact, sometimes R.J.'s progress caught us completely by surprise. There was a point when R.J. was about seven when he realized that he might be able to get in ten more minutes of video game playing before bed because we were tired. After a long day, we sometimes didn't have the energy to go through one of these going-to-bed ordeals with him. So, after our usual series of warnings before turning off the video game, we'd see that he was revving up for a meltdown. Upon a closer look, we could also detect a little bit of mischief in his eyes. He knew that a mini-meltdown, or the threat of one, might get him another round at the controller, so he thought he'd give it a try.

This was a lesson to me, this little glimpse of him trying to get the better of me and Holly. R.J. goes through periods when he catches up so quickly after months of seeming stagnation. As a parent, you have to be alert for the moments when your child, just like Chris Brancato's son Luca, is just acting like any other kid trying to put one over on his parents. It was a pretty happy day for me when I shut off that video game and told R.J., just like I tell the other kids, "That's it, R.J. Time for bed. No excuses."

TIPS FOR DISCIPLINE: CLARITY, CONSISTENCY, AND CONSEQUENCES

Now that I'm the father of four children, I've decided that I know a little bit about how to discipline a child, whether that child is on the spectrum or not. What I've found is that the basic principles for disciplining a child with autism are the same as they are for any child—clarity, consistency, and consequences are the most important things. But you do have to amp all of it up a few notches when the child you are disciplining is on the spectrum. I haven't taken these tips from an expert, although along this journey I've been advised by more than a few. These are my own ideas about what works when you're trying to get results. If with a typical child you would be really clear about what you expect, and always consistent about the consequences for the child not doing what he or she is told, then triple that for kids on the spectrum.

Clarity

- Be clear and complete when you want children to do something (or stop doing something). "Stop it!" isn't enough for them to get it. Be specific about the action you want them to stop doing. Say it two or three times.
- Make physical contact with them to ensure that they are engaged as you explain what you expect them to do. Hold on to their hands, shoulders, or legs.
- Eye contact is important, so that you know that children are acknowledging the fact that you have told them what you expect. This can be a struggle with special needs kids, so try your best.
- Repeat the instruction more than once and get a verbal acknowledgment.
- Give plenty of warning. Start a half an hour before you expect children to obey the command. Check back with a reminder fifteen minutes, ten, five, and a few minutes before, to reinforce the message. This will increase the odds that children will comply.

Consistency

- Have a home schedule that you stick to for homework, meal-times, and bedtime. I know parents are tired, but consistent expectations reinforced over time lessen the resistance you meet.
- Rules are rules, even for special needs kids. Enforce them—all of them—rigorously, so that the kids know that you mean business when you tell them to do something.
- Set limits on computer and video game time and make sure they are rigidly enforced. Even play should have its limits.

Consequences

- In working with your child to find his or her internal drivers, you'll learn what activities or foods you can take away as an effective punishment for bad behavior or noncompliance.
- Learn how to handle meltdowns. Tantrums are a part of life for many parents, especially for those with special needs kids. Try to visualize the tantrum as a process and ride it out without it getting the best of you. If you let frustration or anger show, it will make everything worse.
- Seek help in understanding how to soothe your child through a tantrum triggered by a punishment you've im-

posed. Your child needs to understand why he or she is being punished, and that can't happen while the child is screaming and crying. When the tantrum is over, reinforce the idea that you've withdrawn this privilege because of a specific action on the child's part, or the benefit of the punishment will be lost.

• Don't make the punishment too harsh. To be effective, punishment must be swift and short-lived. Special needs children can have a hard time connecting the punishment to the action that triggered it. If you are still withholding a favorite food or activity weeks later, your child probably won't remember why. Punishment disassociated with the action will then seem cruel.

11

FROM BUTTERFLIES
TO BECKHAM

Part of the Team

G rab your bat and ball and let's go!"

Many dads dream of the day when they can play catch with their sons, go one-on-one on the basketball court, or knock off eighteen holes together. I was no different. From the time I found out that one of our twins was a boy, I looked forward to sitting in the stands and yelling, "Go get 'em, R.J.!" like my dad used to when I was in Little League.

Would R.J. have the same burning desire as I had had, to try his hand at all different kinds of sports? He was fast, well coordinated, and tall. As he grew, it became clear that the sports that appealed to him the most were solo sports like swimming and karate. To me, it seemed like a shame that he wasn't interested in team sports. My hope was that he would be able to make friends by being part of a team. But with his autism, it wasn't likely that he could make a real contribution. Children on the spectrum can become confused by the spontaneous movements of their teammates and opponents in the middle of a game. The way they sometimes melt down under pressure doesn't encourage the other kids to make friends with them.

This was frustrating for a father like me. Sports had done so much to help me develop when I was young. I could remember beginning high school and being extremely nervous because there were going to be so many kids I didn't know there. I had some friends, but would the new kids accept me?

Starting football practice before school began took the pressure off. Friendships occurred naturally on the field. There's something unique about the bond you forge with a teammate who is fighting alongside you for a common goal. Even though you may not always like someone or agree with him, you've got to learn to work together if he is on your team. Sports taught me how to work with others and how to deal with the ups and downs of friendship. You go through so much together as a team that the friendships you make there often last a lifetime.

To be a successful member of a team, you need to be disciplined and you need to always be aware of what's going on around you. Playing a team sport with a ball that could do just about anything demands focus and spontaneity. These are all elements that R.J. needed to practice: discipline, scheduling, timing, understanding competition, and the ability to work with other kids. These are skills that would be essential to him for the rest of his life. If he found a team sport that he loved, he'd be able to learn these naturally, without needing some adult standing over him.

With all that in my mind, it was the hardest thing to keep myself from grabbing him and making him play around with a ball to see if any sport held his interest. I had tried that several times when I was going through my denial-fueled I-can-fix-him stage. My results had been mixed, and mostly discouraging. After I put aside my ego, and really opened myself up to understand what autism is, I taught myself not to impose my dreams upon R.J., but let him express his own interests at his own pace. But I couldn't help but keep my hopes in the back of my mind. Would there ever be a moment when R.J. would come to me and say "Dad, I want to play football"? Or baseball? Or soccer?

By the time R.J. was nearly seven years old, he had learned to follow many social cues, improved his listening skills, and was having an easier time completing his schoolwork. We met every improvement he made with joy, more support, constant encouragement, and increased expectations that he was capable of doing even better in the future. Despite my dreams for him, I didn't want to force him too far past his comfort level by making him join a team sport that was above his skill set. I was also a bit concerned that he might get physically hurt if he wasn't paying attention to what was going on. And I worried that the other kids might tease him and pick on him. Despite my hopes, I believed that by sticking with swimming and karate, he was doing what was best for him.

But as it turned out, R.J. really wanted to play.

For years, R.J. had heard the kids at school talk about the team sports they had played over the weekend. As they shared their stories about the games they'd won or lost, he heard the excitement in their voices. R.J. has always wanted and needed to fit in. Sure enough, when he was seven, the day finally came when he said to me, "Dad, I want to play soccer!"

I almost couldn't believe what he was saying. My dream of watching him play had finally come true. I immediately got him all the best gear: shoes, socks, balls, shin guards, etc. I definitely wanted him to look the part. Just looking at all that gear heaped in bags in the family room made me proud. As I thought about all the ways I could help him succeed in this, I started to become frightened. What if he couldn't get it? What if he couldn't understand the coach? What if the coach didn't have a good field side manner? What if the other kids weren't nice to him? *Oh my God! We'd better start practicing on our own before his official first practice. How do I get him ready?* There wasn't enough time! If he had a bad experience, damn! He wouldn't ever want to play again. *What do I do?*

I went to the expert on coaching: my dad. He flat out told me to stop worrying and let him go. Dad said that R.J. had to learn how to succeed and fail on his own. The sooner I let him earn his own successes and failures, the stronger he would become. Dad's advice made me see that I was so concerned about protecting R.J. that I wasn't able to just let him be a kid. Good, bad, laughing, crying, winning, losing—no matter how he was at soccer, he was *my* boy.

I was glad that he chose soccer, because it seemed like the easi-est sport for him to start with. It's fast, but at the eight-year-old level he'd be playing at, it's basically: go kick the ball in the goal. R.J. had always been athletically inclined. He was a fast runner. I wanted to do what I could to help him succeed, so I started work-ing with him on the skills he would need. Getting him to focus was the hard part.

After we signed him up, R.J. and I went out to the backyard with the soccer ball. The problem with keeping him focused quickly became apparent. A fall afternoon in Los Angeles meant hummingbirds whirling through the azaleas and the sound of the filter burbling in the pool. There were many things to catch a young boy's attention.

"R.J.! R.J.! R.J.!" I called. I moved closer. He looked at me. Suc-cess. "This is what's going to happen. The coach is going to get all of you together. He's going to run some drills where you prac-tice kicking the ball, passing it, or scoring a goal. You're going to listen to him and do exactly what he says, the way you used to do what Conrad told you to do."

First, I kicked the ball and R.J. kicked it back. This was some-thing we'd done hundreds of times. I wanted him to start with an exercise that I knew he could do, that didn't involve anything more than basic footwork. If I could get him to attend to that, his mind might not wander.

As soon as I got him kicking the ball back and forth with me, I had to think about the next step. Part of what I wanted to help him with was making a smooth transition from one element to the next. If we spent too much time on an exercise that he enjoyed, he could get stuck there. He'd resist when I tried to get him to move on to the next thing. We'd had our share of meltdowns at the video game controls or when he didn't want to stop bouncing a basketball and come to dinner, but sometimes he'd get so absorbed in what he was doing that it was difficult to get any reaction from him at all. At these times, if you stopped engaging him directly, his mind would retract into that mysterious space almost the minute you turned your head. It was always a struggle to bring him back.

After we'd been kicking the ball for a while, I decided to show him how to dribble.

"Look, R.J., I'm going to show you something new," I said, capturing the ball between my feet. I kicked the ball a little to the right, then a small shot to the left and caught it with the left foot. "This is how you dribble the ball down the field." I kept kicking it that way as I moved down the lawn. I got to the edge and turned around. I'd lost him. He was looking at the clouds, which were chubby and high, moving fast across the sky.

"R.J.! R.J.!"

He didn't look at me. I started back toward him, dribbling the ball the whole way and narrating.

"It's easy like this. The point is not to make big kicks, R.J. The point is to keep control, keep it between your feet and make it so that you can always get it and keep it," I said. "You keep it nice and tight in this zone."

I was coming straight for him.

"And keep your eyes sharp so that no one gets in there and steals it," I said. I gave the ball a tap and it rolled right over his shoes. R.J. looked at the ball. He looked up at me. Did he even connect the ball showing up with my kicking it? The ball was still rolling.

"R.J.! Stop it!"

He looked at me, confused. So many times in his life I'd told him, "Stop it!" I should have been much clearer.

"The ball! Stop the ball, R.J."

He kept looking at me as the ball continued on to the other side of the yard. *Maybe we should do this side by side.* I jogged over to the ball and dribbled it back, coming to a stop alongside him.

"Okay, this is what we do, R.J. R.J.? R.J.!" He was looking at me, but was he seeing me? Did he understand what I was saying? "We're heading to the fence." I pointed to the other side of the yard. He looked up at my arm and followed the point of my finger, coming to rest at the fence. "The best way to get it there is for us to dribble it, like you dribble a basketball. You love to dribble the basketball, don't you, R.J.?"

His eyes indicated yes.

"In soccer, it's the same thing, but you only get to touch the ball with your feet, never with you hands," I said. I volleyed it back and forth quickly between my feet. "Like basketball when you're passing it hand to hand." I kicked it over to him with my right foot nice and slow. He stopped it with his left and it shot back my way.

"Good! Good, R.J.! That's the way. Only keep it between your feet, just your feet, not mine. And we'll head for that side of the yard. To the fence."

I started off toward the fence, but he didn't make any move to follow. I grabbed him by the hand to tug him forward. He leaned forward and took a step next to the ball, which shot toward me. I kicked it back to him and he kicked it forward. We were heading toward the fence! He was getting it! We weren't dribbling. This was more of a passing drill, but I figured I'd take it.

The next day, when we went out to the yard, I said, "Okay, let's start off with passing just like we did yesterday." I rolled the ball his way and it rolled right past him, as if he had no memory of the hour we'd spent in this exact place at this exact time the day before.

Repetition and consistency are the key. I reminded myself not to be attached to the outcome. *He has to get things in his own way. He takes more time to get things than other boys.* All the advice his therapists and teachers had been giving us for his social skills, his schoolwork, and for play also applied to the basic skills he needed to master this sport. I expected that every day would seem like the first day until one day when he would actually get it and retain it. I'd never be able to predict when that would be.

That night, after we put the kids to bed, I realized that these backyard drills weren't going to be enough. I'd have to talk to the coach about R.J. so that he would take extra effort to get him to participate with the rest of the team.

I got to the first practice early and sat down with the coach to explain that R.J. was on the autistic spectrum. I told him that he'd probably have to call R.J.'s name a few times before he'd pay attention. He might not always understand the coach's instructions on the first go-round. Also, his attention would disappear from time to time when the coach put him out on the field. One thing that we had going for us with R.J. was that he wanted to do everything that the other kids did. If the coach and I worked together to keep him focused, maybe by the end of the season he would be able to keep up with the other kids. I also told him I would make the effort to be at every game and work with R.J. in the yard at home to reinforce what the coach taught him at practice.

As we finished our talk, the other kids and their parents started to arrive. There were gobs of kids and twice as many parents. I was concerned that all the people and activity might overwhelm R.J., but when the coach told them to line up, R.J. got up and stood there with the other kids.

This was eight-year-old soccer, a little bit better than controlled chaos. The ball goes here. The ball goes there. Then one of the kids breaks out and tries to score a goal. It's not at all like it is when they get older and begin to set up plays. Sixteen players, eight on eight, were running up and down the field in a wild pack. When all of the teammates were down there at one end, I realized it wasn't eight on eight—it was eight on seven. R.J. was alone at the opposite end looking around, looking down. He picked up a rock and threw it. I started walking the sidelines trying to get him to pay attention to the game. "R.J.! Go down there! You've got to go down there! R.J.! Go! Get the ball!"

At next week's game, there was still way too much going on. Our coach was yelling on our side. The other coach was yelling on the other side. The kids and the parents were screaming. R.J. just checked out. Again, I ran up and down the sidelines yelling at him to help him stay focused. I probably got a better workout than the players.

The kids rotated positions throughout the game. In the second half, the coach told R.J. to play goalie. I was terrified. When he moved to that position, I stood right behind him, at the back of the net. The ball started out on the other end of the field, so I just let him do his thing. I couldn't tell him to pay attention all the time. When we were left alone together, he turned around to face me.

But as the ball got closer I was "Okay, R.J.! Here it comes! Here it comes! Here it comes! Get ready! Get ready! Get ready! Turn around! Turn around! Stand in the middle. Stand in the middle. Get ready! Get ready! Get ready! Here it comes! HERE IT COMES! They're getting ready to kick it! You've got to stop it! GET READY! GET READY! GET READY!"

The ball went right by him and he just stood there. There it goes. Some of his teammates slapped their heads in frustration.

"Man! You've got to get that!"

"Why didn't you get that?"

"You coulda tried!"

R.J. didn't understand why the kids were yelling at him. It was so frustrating. He stood there looking at the ball and he didn't even move to get it.

This was going to be the longest soccer season in the world.

Every week, we'd have our practices in the yard. He would be great when we worked on it one-on-one. I'd say to him, "Okay, stop it. Control it. Dribble it back and forth three times and kick it." He'd do it. Then game day would come, and he would be by himself at the wrong end of the field. Or the ball would somehow be kicked to him, and he'd stand there and watch it go out of bounds. It would break my heart because I knew he wanted to understand what the other kids were saying and do what the team needed, but he couldn't. He just couldn't.

As rough as each game was, we continued to work on his skills in the backyard. Eventually, he seemed less interested in chasing butterflies on the field and more interested in what the team was doing. He would have tiny flashes of *Okay I get it.* The ball would squirt out of a big group of kids and he would kick it all the way down the field. Or he'd run down the field and chase some kid who had the ball and get it away from him. I would be right there, running alongside him as he headed for the goal, screaming as I'd always wanted to scream, "Way to go R.J.!"

But he wasn't anywhere near consistent. Toward the end of the season, when all the kids had improved and were much more focused on winning, it got tougher and tougher for them to let R.J.'s lapses slide. Ninety percent of the kids were great with him, but there were other kids who were like "You're terrible. Why didn't you get that one?" Some of the parents were also way too into their kid's team winning. You couldn't hear it, but you could feel the other parents grumbling, "He doesn't know how to play. We are sure to lose when he's the goalie."

Even though R.J. appeared to be oblivious to these remarks, I was a little embarrassed for him and for us. It was heartbreaking to watch. *It's not worth it,* I started to think. He just wasn't getting it.

Yet whenever I would tell him that he didn't have to play, he would say, "No. I want to. I am on the soccer team. I want to be on the soccer team. I like it."

"Are you sure you want to go to practice? Is soccer something you really want to do?"

"Yeah. I am on the soccer team. I play on the Cyclones."

The week before the last game of the season, Holly and I were both thanking God this was the last one. We had decided not to sign him up for next year. He wasn't really ready for the team sports thing. We also didn't think he was having that much fun. He was much more interested in the idea of being on a team than he was interested in actually doing what you are supposed to do when you're on a team. I was also tired of subjecting him to those negative reactions from his peers. I pledged to continue working with him in the off-season. Holly and I agreed that in a year we'd reevaluate if he should try soccer again.

As we were on our way to the last game, I tried to talk it up to R.J.

"Okay, this is the last game of the season. Do your best. Try to get a goal. You gonna get me a goal today?"

"Yeah, I'm going to get you a goal."

"You have to be aggressive. You gotta be aggressive, R.J., if you want to score that goal. This is your last chance."

"All right. All right."

As it was the last game, there was a lot of energy on the field. The kids were making lots of shots and both teams were scoring well. At the end of the last half, the score was five to five. The ball stayed down at the other team's goal. R.J. was down there with them, but he didn't have any real shots at the goal.

There were a bunch of kids, as always, scrambling for the ball, when suddenly, it caromed out right toward R.J. He kicked it hard with his left foot. Then time bent for me. It was as if the rest of the commotion on the field had dissolved into a blur as my eyes zoomed in on the soccer ball as it rolled over the yard markers in slow motion right toward the goal. The other kids scrambled, a fury of cleated feet in white socks digging into the turf as the ball slanted in at exactly the right trajectory. SCORE!

You talk about pandemonium. He stood there for a minute as the whole place erupted. The other kids on the team went crazy around him. I was jumping up and down. More than that, the whole side—all filled with parents—were going nuts, going absolutely insane. Then R.J. understood what was happening. He started running back down the field right toward me with a big smile on his face.

For me, it continued to feel as if all of it was taking place in slow motion. He ran down the field with his teammates patting him on the back, but he was locked in on me. He wanted to give his dad a hug. It was like the film *Rudy*, where thousands of people were cheering in the stands but the only ones Rudy saw were his loved ones.

The confidence R.J. gained here made it a major turning point in his life. I played that little movie of him kicking that goal over and over again in my mind, and I think it played in his head too. He could access that incredible feeling of triumph when his teammates rushed toward him to hug him. R.J., the guy they'd dissed and complained about all season, had come through in the clutch and surprised everyone—including himself. Everywhere he looked, every face he saw, beamed joy and success at R.J., the star, the guy who saved the game and saved the season.

He was more communicative after that, he talked about that game often, and he spoke about it clearly. He described it and used words and phrases in a way that I'd never heard him use them before. Both Holly and I believed scoring that goal had unlocked something in him. After that triumphant day, R.J. would constantly ask me how I felt when he scored.

"Dad, remember I scored that goal? Remember I scored that goal?

"How'd you do it, R.J.?"

"I kicked it with my left foot. I kicked it with my left foot."

"Yeah, it was great. Everybody was happy."

"Everybody was happy! Were you happy?"

When he asked, I would relive the moment with him. In my best Al "Do you believe in Miracles?" Michaels's voice, I'd narrate that moment.

"R.J. gets caught up in the struggle for the ball, his team desperately needing a goal. They were so close. The ball was near the other team's goal. All they needed was a clear kick. There were so many defenders around the ball, getting a clean shot would be impossible.

"AND THEN, as if he knew something the other kids didn't, R.J. broke from the pack. And, as if he willed it to happen, the ball squirted out his way. Without hesitation, the ball came right to him. And with the *left* foot, he kicks a laser shot right past the goalie. YES! The crowd goes wild! But Dad goes crazy!"

I couldn't have been more proud of him. His concentration and intensity were things I hadn't seen from him before. I was excited that he scored the goal, but more excited that he understood how great it felt. My boy can do anything!

I just had to hold out for that goal. I realize now that that's what R.J. needed for me to do for him. As tough as it was to watch him struggle through that soccer season and stand on the sidelines with parents who wished he was playing for the other team, I learned that you have to be right there with your kid, and be ready to fight for him no matter what. Regardless of his ups and downs, his faults and his successes, you have to be there for him. The first thing he did after that triumph, the first person he wanted to say something to, was me.

All that time he was trying to make his dad proud, but he didn't know how to do it.

He's going to write a book someday and I'm sure he will say, "When I was growing up, I could see the frustration on my dad's face when I couldn't get something that he wanted me to get, but I showed him I could make him proud."

I don't know how to express to him that I was proud of him anyway. I would have been proud of him if he hadn't scored the goal. I am proud of him no matter what.

TIPS FOR SUCCESS

I think that the reason most fathers want their children to play sports is that it lays a great foundation for life. A father normally leads his child into sports by starting to play games in the back-yard and then gradually using that to get his son or daughter interested in joining a team. But the process isn't so linear with a special needs kid. You could work on a sport with your child for years and never get to the point where that child is ready to join a team. Practice for the child is to learn the skills of the sport, and practice for the dad is to learn to manage your expectations so that the experience is a success for both of you.

Remember that the goal isn't to turn your child into the next Kobe Bryant; it's about finding an enjoyable activity that helps with motor coordination, and using that experience to learn more about what makes your child tick. When your child finds some-thing he or she loves to do, your child will start communicating better, with improved cognitive skills.

Thinking back to that first season with R.J., I realized how much I had learned that might be helpful for other dads.

• ADJUST YOUR EXPECTATIONS TO FIT YOUR CHILD: Sports are about opening up your child's mind and keeping him focused. That's the win, not how many goals he scores or home runs he hits.

• REDEFINE PATIENCE: Whatever your idea of patience is, double that.

• PRACTICE THE SPORT BEFORE THE SEASON BEGINS: This gives your child a better shot at success. He can master the necessary athletic skills, and you can help him practice making the transition from one task to another.

• BREAK THE DRILLS UP: Let your child have free time to run around and do what he wants, including some time to "stim." A good way to keep him engaged is by constantly changing activities. Remember that there are always going to be distractions, and you're sometimes going to have to bring your child back to the task at hand by regularly staying in his face.

• NOTICE WHEN YOUR CHILD IS GETTING OVER-LOADED AND PULL BACK: If you push too much, it's counterproductive. Overload causes a meltdown, and your child can't learn anything in that state.

• DON'T TRY TO REASON DURING A MELTDOWN: I often made that mistake. All R.J. would hear was white noise. This is as true during practice as it is for the game. Massaging his hands, feet, or back did the trick. That physical contact would calm him down, and after that, he could get back in the game.

• GET TO KNOW THE COACH: Let him know that your child needs extra attention and that he should have different expectations for your child's success. Having the coach fully informed and on board with you increases the chances your child will be accepted by the team.

• MAKE FRIENDS WITH THE OTHER PARENTS: We made it a point to let every parent know about R.J. This was probably more important for me than it was for R.J., because I would have been in several altercations if I'd heard a parent talking about my son in the wrong way. One thing I've learned is that people respond better to you and your child when you are open and honest.

• ATTEND EVERY GAME: If he's committed, you have to commit too. He needs you at his side to succeed.

• CELEBRATE VICTORIES, NO MATTER HOW SMALL: It's easy to be disappointed if your child isn't as good as the other kids, but if you step out of your world and see things through your child's eyes, you'll no longer feel disappointed. Compliment him on a good block or a strong kick that shows he was paying attention and so were you. From your child's perspective, this is as important as scoring a goal.

• FIND THOSE TEACHABLE MOMENTS: There is a lesson in everything your child does, and it is up to you to find that meaning and reinforce it. If R.J. was playing goalie and the ball got past him, we would talk about that after the game. We'd replay that moment together, and I'd get him to visualize it. When he could see the ball, he could imagine kicking it. This was a great way to explain to him that the key to success in that position is to watch the ball the entire time. To see him apply that lesson even once or twice in the next practice or game was the most amazing thing.

• DISCOVER WHAT MOTIVATES YOUR CHILD: Different things drive different kids. The unstructured play of sports is a chance to spend time with your child and discover what motivates and excites him. Once you figure that out and embrace whatever it is, the communication between you will be ten times better.

12

MAKING FRIENDS

A common worry for many dads is that their children won't have any friends. Friends are as important as family in shaping a child's concept of who he is and what is possible for him. R.J. knows that we love him and that he can depend on us to stand by him no matter what, but building friendships with his peers was probably the biggest hurdle he would face. We could tutor him on his schoolwork, get him to rub up against his siblings at home, but we couldn't force the kids at school to include him.

One of the things we liked most about the school we chose to enroll R.J. in was its strong emphasis on tolerance and acceptance. The teachers taught those principles right alongside math, science, and reading. The Lab School drew its students from all of Los Angeles and tried to represent every part of society's spectrum, so that the student body would be a reflection of the city as a whole. The teachers frequently talked to the students about individuality and how everyone was different, with different weaknesses and strengths. At every grade level, the lessons included asking the children to consider how the whole class benefited from combining the qualities of all the students, reinforcing the fact that all of them should be welcomed into the life of the classroom and the school.

This was nicely managed inside the classroom, but the playground was the place that concerned me. We all remember from our own childhoods how brutal kids can be. I was haunted by the memory of R.J. at his first school—the way he would walk the perimeter of the yard alone, turning the water faucet on and off endlessly, and how he was never called in to play games with the other kids or invited to other kids' homes for playdates.

Early on we saw how tough socializing was for R.J. when we would be invited as a family to birthday parties of our friends' children. The average kid's birthday party has a noise level a few decibels lower than an amusement park. In Los Angeles, with its perpetual sunshine, the colors of the banners, balloons, and napkins always seemed brighter than other places. Even I sometimes had a hard time keeping my bearings in the middle of the commotion, so I understood why R.J. often shut down quickly in the midst of it.

And then there was the food issue. We knew that diet had played a big role in R.J.'s condition. He was allergic to wheat and dairy, and we didn't like what happened when he got too much sugar in him. What's the menu at almost every kid's birthday party? Pizza, cake, and ice cream. A gluten/casein smorgasbord! Every bite of it was forbidden.

Holly was really good about searching out places to buy gluten-free pizza and cake for us to bring along so that R.J. could in his own way enjoy what the other kids were having. This stayed with me though, this idea of him being there but not fully included.

Kids are so sensitive about being different from their peers—from listening to the right music to wearing the right clothes. When the kids were really young, none of their peers noticed that R.J. ate separate food. But I expected that by the time R.J. got to the end of elementary school, the other kids would start noticing these differences, and if we didn't handle this situation well, he would be embarrassed about it. We knew right from the beginning that it was essential we mainstream him socially as well as academically.

R.J.'s academic challenges required that he have a full-time aide who could help him stay on task in the classroom and help guide him through the transitions from one subject to another. A well-trained aide tries to fade into the background as much as possible so that the other kids don't notice that Mr. Mark or Mr. Tim is there specifically to help R.J.

In the early years, Mark's approach was to go easy on the academics during the school day and then make up for what R.J. missed when they got home that afternoon. If Mark made the fact that he was helping R.J. too obvious, it would further isolate him socially, because all the other kids could see that R.J. was a little slower and took the world in differently. R.J. was always his number one priority, but Mark also helped the other students in the class in order to make his focus on R.J. less conspicuous. As a result, the teachers in R.J.'s classes got lucky. They ended up with someone else in the room who could help them keep the class in order. Both of R.J.'s aides ended up doing this, helping the entire class, especially the boys.

This was a little bit harder for them to negotiate on the playground. If Mark or Tim was hanging around R.J. all the time, none of the other kids would spontaneously include him in their games. Mark decided that the best way to get R.J. included was to be the one who organized the games, a tradition that Tim followed.

Sometime around second grade, Mark steered R.J. to handball, which ended up being a huge boost to his social life. This wasn't the kind of handball that adults play, in a wooden court with rackets and protective eyewear. The kids played against a wall outside the classroom with a big ball that was similar in color to a basketball but not as hard. As soon as the recess bell rang, they dashed to that wall to line up.

It took a while for R.J. to understand the rules, so in the beginning Mark had to hang around and make sure he stayed in the game. You start playing when you get to the head of the line, and you go to the back of the line as soon as you lose. If you keep winning, you keep playing—your opponent becomes the next person in line, then the person after that person, and so on. Learning how to take turns and how to wait was important to the game. We had had a tough time with R.J. tackling these issues, but because he was older now and because this was something he wanted to do, he was able to pick up on it without too much coaching. Once he got the hang of rules of the game and waiting in line, he could play with the others kids without any adults around. This was exactly the kind of benefit we wanted R.J. to get from friendship: a social success that he could be proud of on his own.

When kids are that young, their friendships aren't about personal confessions or supporting one another through tough times. The boys just stand around in the same space and, during handball, shout out about what's going on in the game. This was a great way for R.J. to develop a friendship, because he didn't have to talk much. And it certainly helped that he was a good player right off the bat.

Once Mark and R.J. told me how much this game meant to him, I wanted to do everything I could to help him. Nights after dinner, we'd play up against the garage door. At first, I'd let him win and then complain long and hard about how he robbed me— which he really enjoyed. And it wasn't too long before I wasn't pretending about that anymore.

Suddenly he had all these trash-talk phrases for naming the different shots. One of his best moves was a hard, low shot that skipped across the pavement. The kids called that one a "slicey." They also had a rule, like in tennis, about the winner getting two tries to serve the ball. If the first serve went out of bounds, R.J. called it a "first bad."

He very quickly picked up this language all on his own because it mattered to him that he be just like the other boys. His status in the group went up, and he looked forward to recess, which was one of the few times of the school day when he didn't have to be prompted by Mark or the teachers to get into the mix. Again, this was a social success he could claim all for himself.

We always made a big deal out of the twins' birthday parties, inviting everyone in the class and their parents to a day at a fun place like Universal Studios. For two weeks, R.J. would be the coolest kid in the class, but then that memory would fade and R.J.'s status would decline. We noticed that Ryan would get invited to the birthday parties of every one of the girls in her class, but we'd hear about birthday parties for boys and know that R.J. wasn't getting invited.

Holly isn't the kind of person to let something like this rest. Soon after we realized this, the school had an open house night for just the parents and the teachers. After the teacher made her presentation, Holly asked to address the class.

"For those of you who do not know, R.J. is on the autistic spectrum," she said. "He's come a long way and I want you to know he is a great kid. Just like your kids, he wants to be included. He wants to go to birthday parties and playdates. So don't be shy about asking him, because we know he'd be happy to go."

Many of the parents thanked us for that afterward. I was proud of Holly for getting up there and speaking. Admitting something like that in front of people you don't know well takes a lot of courage. Some families keep autism a secret, and the fact that Holly wasn't going to be shy about it made me think R.J. was going to have a great year socially.

Then nothing happened.

Well, something happened, but it wasn't a good thing.

Mark was in the yard one day, and he saw R.J. surrounded by a bunch of kids from his class. They were all laughing hysterically. A few of the kids were holding their sides. There was R.J. right in the middle. Mark edged over to the group quietly to see what was going on without disturbing the scene. What he heard shocked him. The kids were prompting R.J. to say foul words like "poop" and "dookie." He was going along with it without knowing what he was saying. Mix in his echolalia—the endless repeating of a phrase—and he was like a real live windup toy, repeating it over and over.

On one level, R.J. felt like this was a big success. He was the center of attention, getting a big reaction, even though he didn't really know what was so funny. Of course, on another level, it was heartbreaking that they were exploiting his vulnerabilities, as kids sometimes do. Mark made sure the boys who had done this were all counseled by the teacher. That afternoon, he had a long discussion with R.J. about what words were okay and what words weren't okay, without specifically mentioning what had happened that afternoon.

Then Mark told us, and we realized what it really meant that R.J. had "crossed the bridge."

The school is built on the edge of a small ravine with a creek running through it. The lower grades stay in the lower yard, where the play structures are smaller, the right size for kids under the age of eight. As the students move toward the end of third grade, they get focused on how they are just about to move to the upper yard, to "cross the bridge" over the creek to where the big kids play.

We thought of this as just a geographical shift, but it was more than that. Fourth grade is a time when the school starts demanding real thinking from kids. Their minds are maturing, and they can handle more complicated tasks, like synthesizing information from different sources and writing reports. Their social lives get more complex too. They're not standing side by side at the handball court anymore. They're drawing lines between themselves, choosing sides. The power of groups is so strong that it was possible that the boys who had been his friends in the lower grades would decide that continuing to be friends with R.J. was uncool. This was a time when, if we didn't handle this just right, R.J. could get marginalized.

First, we talked to R.J., but we knew right away that we weren't getting through to him on this subject. When we mentioned kids at school we knew were getting picked on, R.J. named another boy who he thought was having a rough time. But he didn't put himself in that category. I guessed that Mark was doing a pretty good job—he had managed to educate R.J. about the words he shouldn't be saying without letting him catch on to the fact that the boys who surrounded him that afternoon were not treating him very well.

"You wouldn't pick on kids," I said. "And you wouldn't like to be picked on, would you?"

"No, I don't pick on kids," he said. "That's mean. No one picks on me."

We knew that talking to the parents of his classmates wasn't enough. After Holly had spoken up at parents' night, there was a brief increase in R.J.'s invitations to play at other kids' houses, but that had already died down. The kids are the ones who make the invitations, and the parents just go along with it. Their good intentions from parents' night were long forgotten by the time we'd entered November. We knew they couldn't be hovering over their boys on the playground every day either. We decided we had to speak to the kids directly about R.J.'s autism.

We sat down with R.J.'s teachers and the school's psychologist, Dr. Jeff Jacobs, to see if they thought this was a good idea or if it might just make a bad situation more difficult. Both of them agreed this was a great idea. Dr. Jacobs told us that he thought the kids needed more information, not less. If the kids knew what was going on with R.J., then they wouldn't be confused. Dr. Jacobs felt that knowledge would help engage their compassion.

But it was up to us to figure out what to tell them.

So we asked our resident expert on the politics of the fourth grade, Ryan, to help us.

Ryan is that typical young girl who can act like a whiny toddler one minute and a college freshman the next. Although it was clear how much she loved her brother, when she was younger and R.J. was more withdrawn, she used to refer to him as her "invisible twin." She had a twin, but he wouldn't play with her. While it was her nature to watch after him anyway, she also felt that R.J. was her special responsibility. Though they were in separate classes most of the time, the other kids sometimes asked, since she and R.J. were twins, if Ryan had autism too. With all this history in mind, Ryan jumped at the chance to help set the record straight with her peers. She was profound and amazing.

"Don't say anything that will embarrass R.J.," she said to start off.

"Well, like what?" I asked.

"Don't say the word 'autism' more than once or twice," she advised.

Holly and I looked at each other. That would be a neat trick: to talk about something for an hour or so without really mentioning it.

"What are we supposed to call it then?" Holly asked.

Ryan looked a little exasperated, as if she was dealing with dummies.

"Call it autism, but don't keep using that word," she said in a very impatient voice. "If you say it a bunch of times and they remember it, then they'll have a label for R.J. He'll be the autistic boy. He won't be R.J. anymore."

Whoa! My sentiments exactly. Except these were the sentiments I'd had before I accepted the fact that R.J. was on the spectrum.

"Then we won't have that much to talk about if we're avoiding that subject," I said.

"No! You're not avoiding the subject. You're explaining it, only without the labels. You talk about differences. That's where you start. Everybody is different. Some of them do some things well and some of them do other things well. R.J. is a kid with weaknesses too. Everyone has weaknesses. Then when you talk about the things he can't do, they can see how he is just like them, only a little different."

I looked over at Holly. She was taking notes.

"Don't just talk about what he can't do," Ryan continued. "R.J. can do some amazing things. You have to tell them what they are. Otherwise they'll only be thinking he's got something wrong with him. There are a lot of things that are right with R.J."

"Shouldn't we be talking about his brain and how it works so they can understand why he is the way he is?" I asked the professor.

"Sure, but really don't spend too much time on that," Ryan said. "Tell them how maybe he has some trouble looking people in the eye or answering when he's called."

"Right, and then I can explain how he gets overstimulated and has to shut down because it's too much for him. He can't process it all," I suggested.

"I don't think so, Dad," Ryan said. "Don't say 'processing.' Don't give them too much information. They're only interested in the things about R.J. that affect how he can be their friend. You want to explain the things he does that they don't understand as coming from the way his brain works. Almost all the time his brain works fine. He's really nice to everyone. When he likes kids, he likes them for who they are, not for the sneakers they are wearing or the cool thing their parents just gave them. That's important. That's really important."

The next day, when Holly and I went to address the class, we were sweating. R.J. and Ryan had agreed they didn't want to be around for this talk, so it was just me and Holly up there. We weren't sure how the class would react or how we'd be able to handle it if they were cold to us or made fun of us or R.J. I've played stadiums in front of 90,000 screaming fans, and I'd take that any day over trying to explain autism to a classroom of fourth graders. Unfortunately, this is the age when cynicism starts to creep into kids' minds. As we walked up to the front of the class, I noticed that several of them were leaning back in their chairs with their arms folded. *Show me!*

"How many of you have heard of the word 'autism'?" Holly said to start off. Most of the class raised their hands.

Okay, I was thinking, *she said it once. We've got one more left.*

"How many of you know a child who has it?"

All the hands went down to their laps.

"You can put your hands back up, because R.J. has it."

"Do any of you know what having it means?" I asked. *Nice,* I thought. I managed to ask the question without saying that word again.

"What that means is that his brain is wired in a different way, and because of that, it's harder for him to communicate. So talking to people, starting off a conversation, is something that R.J. isn't very good at. Have any of you noticed that R.J. doesn't come up to you very much?"

We saw kids scattered around the room nodding their heads in agreement.

"Most of you do that all the time and don't even think about it because it's not hard for you. That's very, very hard for R.J., but it doesn't mean that he doesn't want to talk to you. I bet if we went around the room here, every one of you could say that you are good at some things and not so good at others, couldn't you?" Holly asked.

"I'm good at soccer," one boy said. "But I suck at math."

"I can ride my dirt bike really fast, even on a muddy track," said another. "But I'm not doing so great in Spanish class."

"Guess what? R.J. can tell you the name of every president and vice president of the United States in order," Holly said.

"And he can tell you the name of every single active player on every team in the NFL or the NBA. Even the NHL," I said. "But making friends is really hard for him."

"Sometimes when you call him, he won't answer," Holly continued. "You have to call him more than once because that's just how long it takes for him to get the message."

"Really?" asked one of the girls. "I thought that was because he didn't like me."

"Yeah," said a boy from the other side of the room. "I thought he was ignoring me because he didn't want to play with me."

"No, he does want to play with you," Holly said. "That's the most important thing to him. And if you're his friend, he'll always like you for exactly who you are, not for the sneakers you're wearing."

By the end of our talk, it was like a lightbulb had gone on in all of their heads. We were so surprised by how well that went. As we were driving home in the car, we couldn't get over what we had learned in that little bit of time we'd spent with the kids. It had never occurred to us that they might feel R.J. didn't like them! We always thought they were the ones rejecting him.

As frightening as it was for us to address the class, the big chance we took paid off immediately. We got e-mails from a few of the other parents the next night, reporting that their kids had come home and asked them how to spell autism so that they could look it up on the Internet. The number of playdates and invitations to parties increased. While he'll probably never get as many as Ryan, R.J. doesn't need as many as she does. He just needs a few kids who understand him and want to include him.

While our talk had definitely been a success, I was concerned that it would be a onetime thing, with only a temporary effect on R.J.'s relationships with the other kids in the class. You never know how much kids are going to retain and how friendships are going to shift as they get older. R.J. still needs some help to get it right socially. But he's being given more help now.

Hanging around in the yard before school, the boys usually talked about sports. Tim Lee was standing on the edge of one of these conversations where the kids were talking about a football game from that Sunday. R.J. wanted to be included in the conversation. He asked the group if they'd seen the UCLA basketball game. The conversation stopped.

Tim wanted to show R.J. how to plug himself into the mix in an appropriate way by subtly pointing out how to talk about what the other kids were discussing. "Rodney, didn't you watch that game? Didn't you see that touchdown?"

Tim told us that the recognition swept over R.J.'s face.

"Yeah, that was in the third quarter," he said.

"I saw that too," one of the other kids said.

"He was number twelve and he threw a pass that was for forty yards," R.J. added.

Tim said the other kids were impressed. "Whoa, how did you know that?" one said. He was just one of the guys.

R.J. has a friend, a confident guy and a good athlete, who makes sure to sit next to him in class and gives him a little nudge when he sees that R.J.'s mind has started to wander away from the subject the teacher is explaining. The kids do that at lunch too, reminding R.J. that he's got to eat his lunch, because he can sometimes forget. The schoolyard's not the kind of place where other kids always need to watch out for R.J., though. One thing he's really proud of is that the status he earned in kickball has stayed. He's always among the first kids picked when they are choosing sides for basketball or baseball. When the older kids organized a flag football team, R.J. was the only fourth grader they invited. They're not doing that out of the kindness of their hearts—they're doing that because they want him on the team.

I recently took R.J. to a birthday party for one of his classmates. Of course, Robinson wanted to go and kept pestering R.J. to bring him. R.J. brushed him off. "These are *my* friends, Robinson," he said. "I want to see them without you."

The party was at the ESPN Zone, which was a madhouse of noise and lights and motion. R.J. handled it fine. He had his friends around him. When it was time for the cake, the mom called out for them to gather around, but R.J. was still playing on a video game. One of the kids called him again, but R.J. didn't hear. Eventually one of his friends left the place where they were about to cut the cake and walked over to R.J. to touch him on the shoulder.

"Rodney," he said. (R.J. is currently trying to get people to call him Rodney.) "It's time to eat over there."

I watched the kids around him now and saw how they embraced him. They understand him and they take care of him. When I say "take care," I don't mean that they baby him. They get him. They include him, because that's what friends do.

TIPS FOR MAKING FRIENDS

• LET EVERYONE KNOW: The school will know that your child has autism, but their schoolmates and their parents must know too. Being embarrassed or secretive about it further isolates your child and doesn't give the others a chance to extend a hand. Explain your child's limitations, verbal or otherwise.

• TALK IN A LANGUAGE KIDS UNDERSTAND: When you talk about autism to the other kids, make sure that you describe it in terms that are not over their heads. Ryan was absolutely right in telling us to first think about how R.J.'s condition affects the other kids, instead of focusing on how it feels to him. Avoid medical terms and long words—that's the fastest way to get kids to tune out. The kids who want to know more will be able to read about it on their computers that night, just like the kids in R.J.'s class did.

• REMIND THE PARENTS YOUR KID HAS SOCIAL NEEDS TOO: Don't be shy about encouraging other families to invite your child along. I realize that this might seem awkward, and a little embarrassing, but it's your child's social life we're talking about here, not yours. A little nudge from you might get a parent to invite your child over, and a new friendship might take root from that invitation.

• MAKE SURE THE OTHER PARENTS KNOW YOUR CHILD'S ROUTINE: You want any playdate or outing to be a success, so that your child will be asked back. To make this possible, the other parents have to be fully informed of the things that set your child off. If loud noises are a problem, make sure that the other parents know this. If your child has a special diet, pack lunch and snacks. The other family is doing a wonderful thing for your child, and you must bring them up to speed to make sure this experience goes as smoothly as possible.

• BE GENEROUS ABOUT INVITING OTHERS: Playdates, sleepovers, trips to the movies, and birthday parties are chances for you to help your child build some rapport with others in his or her class. Take every opportunity to boost your child's social life.

• CREATE "FAMILY" PLAYDATES: If you put together an afternoon event and invite one of your child's friend's family along, the other parents can see how you interact with your child. This may take some of their hesitation away and can expand your child's social possibilities.

• PARTICIPATE IN SCHOOL OUTINGS: Driving a group of kids in a car pool to the museum or going on a nature hike with the class gives you a chance to watch the way your child fits in with peers. This can help you understand where your child needs a little coaching. You might also identify a potential new friend in the group.

• PRACTICE SKILLS THAT WILL HELP YOUR CHILD SOCIALLY: My time practicing kickball and basketball with R.J. was fun for both of us, and it was also good for him socially. I helped him build confidence in his skills for these games, which made him a better player and a more valuable member of the team. Help with your child's interests as much as you can. In doing so, you'll help your child lay the foundation for success with his or her peers.

13

THE OTHER SPECTRUM

When we speak about our children with autism, we talk about "kids on the spectrum." But there's another spectrum to consider—the financial spectrum. Autism hits families at all levels of income, yet getting your child with autism everything he needs is incredibly expensive, and very little of those costs are covered by health insurance. Holly and I estimate that we spent at least $160,000 a year on the different therapies, services, unconventional medical treatments, and aides for R.J. in the early years of our journey with autism. I know this is an incredible amount of money. It probably sounds completely ridiculous to you if you are unfamiliar with what it costs to really help a child with serious special needs.

Holly and I count ourselves extremely lucky that we were able to afford those important services for R.J. on our own, but no matter what resources your family has, the most important thing to understand about "the other spectrum" is that you do have options.

Federal law requires that every child in this country be allowed a "free and appropriate public education." If your public school system isn't able to meet your child's needs, then it is obligated to fund his or her education at a private school that is equipped to challenge and nurture children on the spectrum. There is often friction between parents and a school system about exactly what constitutes "appropriate" education. What a parent sees as appropriate might seem outrageous to a cash-strapped school district. Parents often find themselves squared off against a sprawling bureaucracy with impenetrable procedures that are designed to intimidate families and keep them from asking for what their child needs. Parents often even have to sue the school district in order to make it cough up the resources that a child on the spectrum is entitled to.

Suing may seem like an extreme step, but it is frequently the only way parents can get real, meaningful help for a child. With as many as 1 in 100 children on the spectrum in some parts of the country, these legal cases have become so common that some lawyers dedicate their entire practice to them. (If you do not have a lot of money and if you cannot get the services your child needs through the local school system, a lawyer who specializes in these cases may take on your child's case without requiring a legal fee up front—the special education lawyer will then deduct your fee from any money you get from the school district.)

All parents want to do anything and everything they can for their children. When you hear from a friend about a new kind of machine that has improved a child's speech, it's natural to want to leap at that chance for your child. You can't help but think that maybe this new machine is the secret to getting your child to speak again. But when the money is not available and the family credit cards are maxed out, how do you decide which therapies you need to let go of? It can be incredibly difficult to make these decisions without the help of other people who are advocates for your child.

I've seen a lot of struggles against bureaucracy in the years I've spent getting to know families of children with autism, but none of the struggles compared to what Khari Lee had to go through for his son. Khari faced a huge fight as a lone man against the state, while struggling to manage an equally important fight that raged within himself.

I first met Khari when I started taking R.J. to Smart Start. Smart Start encouraged parents to stay in the classroom with their children for the first forty-five minutes every morning in order to help the children make the transition into the school day. The only other dad who'd be in the room at that time was Khari, a man who stands out everywhere he goes (he's more than six feet tall). Like me, Khari lingered after the time came for the parents to leave. When I hung back in the hallway, peering through the tiny window of the schoolroom door to see how R.J. was doing without me, Khari's face was always pressed against the window next to mine. Soon, a friendship was struck between two men on opposite sides of "the other spectrum."

Khari is a big man, but he carries himself like a cat. He wears loose jeans and big, baggy T-shirts. The back of his denim jacket, which is cut more like a trench coat than a bomber jacket, has a full-length drawing of a tough, muscular male physique with a pit bull head on it. Khari's moves are fluid, but his demeanor is wary. His eyes are almost always walled off behind his shades, even when he's indoors. Unable to make direct eye contact through his glasses, my gaze tended to stray to the deep red knife scar across the right side of Khari's neck, a token from his time as a member of the Bloods, one of the most notorious gangs in Los Angeles. Khari was not the kind of guy I usually saw in the predominantly female world of special education. "No teacher who ever went to school to learn how to teach special education thought she was going to have to deal with me," Khari would say with a wry smile.

There's a hint of delight in the way Khari describes his handling of interactions in these rooms, rooms where there are many assumptions about the way that polite people are supposed to behave. When Khari goes in to negotiate with the staff at his son's school, he knows that most people quickly sign off on their child's individualized education program or IEP. The language in those forms can be confusing, and the parents are usually outnumbered by the administrators, psychologists, and teachers arrayed on the other side of the conference table. But Khari always takes his time, never having been the kind of man who assumes that the authorities have the best interests of his son in mind. He's always suspicious that there is some other therapy, some better school, or some fund of cash that they haven't told him about. Some families might hire a lawyer to help them protect their rights and make sure they're getting everything their child is entitled to. Others might do what they can to pay for therapies out of their own money. But Khari uses what he's got: the fact that he's intimidating.

Khari moved with his mom from New Jersey to Los Angeles when Khari was five years old, so his mom could take a job in public relations. Khari became a latchkey child who fell into the gang life when he was in high school. He was always a reliable solider in street fights—the kind of guy you'd want to have next to you.

He shielded his mom from the knowledge that he was in a gang until one night when he was seventeen. That night, he came home with the blood of his best friend—a boy his mother had known since she and Khari first moved to LA—smeared on his arm. "A lot of males in Los Angeles play Russian roulette with their lives," Khari recalls. Although Khari says he would never steal, sell drugs, do drugs, or prey on the weak, he admits that he had dark days that were filled with trouble. He estimates he's buried more than twenty of his friends. "I was violent. My friends knew that, and that was a way I gained respect. But there was a line I would not cross."

Considering how he was living, Khari didn't expect to be around past the age of twenty-one. When his girlfriend got pregnant, he realized that he needed to change his life to support his son. He'd enrolled in a trade school and was learning how to be a professional chef when he noticed that his son wasn't developing as quickly as he should have been. After Khari Jr.'s measles/

mumps/rubella vaccinations, the boy stopped communicating. "My son left," Khari said. "He just left. His spirit left." Khari Sr. and Khari Jr.'s two grandmothers raised the money to get the boy tested at UCLA. The doctor said that Khari Jr. was on the spectrum. Khari Sr. immediately quit school. "My life kinda went on hold and it's been on hold ever since." That was a decade ago.

Khari and his son's mom had been distant from each other ever since the baby was born. The mother never seemed to bond with Khari Jr. When the baby was released from the hospital soon after his birth, he lived with Khari Sr.'s mom, not his own biological mom. The mom used to visit Khari Jr. a few times a week, but that stopped after the diagnosis. Khari developed this overwhelming sense that he was the only person who could help his son, and he was going to fight for him with every ounce of energy he had.

But at the same time, Khari wondered if his strong feelings would really do his son any good.

"I know me. It was definitely going to be the H word. I was either going to help my son or hinder my son," he said. "I am going to be dealing with schoolteachers and principals, and I know how they are going to look at me. They'll look at me the same way they've always looked at me. I thought I needed to go to school."

Khari started to study autism and its treatments the way he'd never studied in school. Those subjects hadn't mattered to him the way this one did. He attended seminars on occupational therapy, physical therapy, and speech. He traveled fifty miles on a weekend to attend a graduate school seminar on autism and the tongue in Orange County. "My son doesn't speak, and he doesn't eat," Khari said. "He needs the same set of muscles for both tasks, but he can't get them moving in the right way."

When he walked through the door of the pastel-and-brass hotel conference room, he could see the graduate students and professors instantly tense up. "At first they were looking at me like, Who is this black man asking all these questions?" he said with a smile. "But I had already taken all these classes and there were specific things I wanted to know. Once they saw it was a genuine passion for me, they got over me quick."

The more Khari learned about his son's condition, the further and further it took him from gang life. The sense of family that gang life had given him suddenly looked weak and false when he had a real family crisis to manage. Only a few of his friends from the Bloods were interested in talking to him about his son. Also, for the first time in his life, Khari recognized that someone was utterly dependent on him. He realized that "I've got to come home every day. I can't run in those circles where I might not be safe, or I might have to do something risky." He cut his ties to the gang in order to devote himself full-time to helping his son.

I don't know how many men would even consider becoming a full-time advocate, much less succeed at it, but Khari's results speak for themselves. In his initial attempts, he was able to get a significant amount of services for his son paid for by the Los Angeles Unified School District. This is not an easy thing to do.

Mark Woodsmall, a Los Angeles lawyer who specializes in advocating for the rights of children with special needs, draws an interesting contrast between what the demanding parents on the city's affluent west side secure for their children and what poor families on the east side receive for theirs. "The children on the west side routinely get private sessions in applied behavioral analysis paid for by the district, but that's unheard of in the south and east, the poorer parts of town," Woodsmall said.

In the course of tutoring his son so that he could learn and grow, Khari had to learn and mature in ways that he had believed were out of his reach. I've seen fathers go through an identity crisis when fatherhood doesn't turn out exactly as they pictured it would be. Most of us make an adjustment and move on. But Khari had to find a way to change his whole life.

This was extremely clear the day the regional center sent a specialist over to the house to teach Khari floortime. "You have to remember my mentality, where I come from, is What is this clown doing playing with my son on the floor? What are you doing, homie? You irritating me, sitting there playing. Then I started to realize that it wasn't his job to explain himself to me. He was trying to help us all out. He was trying to help me understand my son. I had to take a step back, and when I did I saw that he wasn't even intimidated by me. I respected him for doing what he was doing; he didn't care about the attitude I was throwing him," Khari said.

The realization that people were willing to help him, and that he and his son needed to accept their help, struck him again. All of this came together when Khari Jr. was at Smart Start.

In every other place, Khari had felt that the administration of the school tried to keep him at bay because he didn't look or act like the other parents. He's not the kind of person you can dismiss: he won't allow it. He is passionate, confrontational, and physically intimidating, but there is no questioning the love and concern he demonstrates every day for his son. Smart Start is very close to Khari's home, so Khari visited the school whenever he felt like it. And he was never made to feel unwelcome. Through letting him work with his son's teachers, the school reclaimed a part of Khari that he'd thought was long gone. They taught him how to play.

Khari Jr. is severely affected by his autism. Although he and Khari Sr. have developed their own way of communicating, even at the age of fourteen he still has very little language. Khari Sr.'s stubbornness and resourcefulness have helped him wrangle a significant number of concessions from the school district. When the services and therapies provided by the school the district had placed his son in didn't seem to be helping, Khari Sr. didn't hesitate to complain about them. His persistence and passion persuaded the district to pay for Khari Jr.'s fees to attend several different private schools and, for two years, got him private home schooling with a specialist. "He made the most progress during the private home schooling," Khari recalls.

Not everyone can call upon Khari's righteous outrage when

dealing with the authorities. Manuel Munguia is in a similar situation to Khari's in that he also needed to ask the school district for help, but he is in the middle range of income, not low income like Khari. He and his wife, Deanna, earn just enough that they can pay for some additional services for Little Manny. But with two other children to support, every dollar has to be stretched to the limit.

"The officials pick and choose who they want to give services to. They give the services to the ones who do not give up, so we're not budging," Manuel said.

Manuel has always been a man able to provide for his family. Having to fight is honorable, but for Manuel, having to beg is unacceptable. He and Deanna watch their money carefully and they got assistance from their large and very generous family for the two years Manuel had to take off work so that he could manage Little Manny's care full-time. "We are seeing progress. We are seeing him start to get it. He can't speak full sentences yet, but he's getting there. If there's a therapy he needs that can get him there, I'll find a way to pay for it. I'll take a second job. I'm embarrassed to say that in the last year and a half we've spent eighty thousand dollars on services for Little Manny."

But while Manuel is willing to fight the world to get his son what he needs, and work two jobs to pay for it, the real thing he believes he needs to do is slow down and listen. This goes against all his male instincts. "To fight the bureaucracy, you have to really know your child," he said. "You have to spend time with him so that you can describe the ways that he is unique and so you know how the cookie cutter they want to force him into doesn't fit his needs. If you really know your child, they can't scare you off with all that jargon they use."

In his latest fight, Manuel is trying to get the district to pay for individualized day care. Manuel has gone back to work full-time because Little Manny is old enough to be in school. Group day care is fine for Manuel and Deanna's two typical girls, but it's not safe for Little Manny, who needs a lot of attention to ensure he doesn't harm himself. He may be improving on many levels, but he still doesn't understand danger. "We are a team on this," Manuel said. "Deanna is emotional. She shows them how much this means for our family. I am the voice of determination and specifics. I explain specifically who he is and why he needs this."

TIPS FOR THE OTHER SPECTRUM

• BUILD A TEAM: As parents, you are at the tip of the spear in the effort to get more support for your child, but you also need to build a team in order to successfully face the bureaucracy. Having experts on your side is the key to bolstering your case for more services. While you might find an advocate or a doctor who is sympathetic to you and your child, you must also establish their reputation with the district. If your representative has lost significant battles with the authorities while advocating for the rights of other families, you go into a negotiation carrying the weight of those other disputes. You want to find advocates and experts who are respected and have a good track record with the people who oppose you in the school district.

· HONEY VS. VINEGAR: When Khari says his involvement can either help or hinder his son, he's touching on a issue that a lot of parents face when they are advocating for their children. Hostility and threats should be the tactics of last resort. In my experience, you go a long way toward creating a positive atmosphere and opening up good possibilities when you start off by saying that you know how everyone in the room wants the best for your child and that you're all working for the same goal. Try to maintain that spirit until this is shown not to be true.

· PERSISTENCE: The wheels of the government move slowly. Never accept your first rejection of services. There is always someone to whom you can appeal a decision.

· KNOW YOUR CHILD: Trust your gut in deciding what your child needs. You spend a lot of time with that child, and your observations, along with the recommendations of your doctor and other specialists, are key in determining what kinds of therapy and treatment will be the most effective. Some districts take a cookie cutter approach to giving services to children with special needs. Only your acute observations of the differences in your child's needs can get the district to address that child as a unique individual whose requirements are truly special. Also, being firm in what you think will work in improving your child's condition means you come from a much stronger negotiating position.

• KEEP GOOD RECORDS: In addition to keeping a thorough file on your child's medical history, you must also keep good records of your interactions with insurance companies and school authorities. This means writing down the result of every phone call, the time it was made, and the person you spoke with. This is particularly important when dealing with insurance companies. One person you speak with on the phone might tell you that the speech therapy you want to begin is covered up to a certain amount. The next day you could get someone who says it's not covered at all. These records are vital both to improve your encounters with the insurance companies and for the sake of your own sanity.

• KNOW YOUR RIGHTS: Knowing what your child is entitled to under the law is important in giving you the courage to persist through tough negotiations. While policies and standards of care vary from state to state and school district to school district, there are some fundamental federal principles that guide all decisions related to your child. Knowing those rights is vital to your success.

14

YOU'RE NOT ALONE

When I started really working to help R.J., I began going with him to his therapies in order to understand his world better and figure out how I could contribute. One of the things I noticed right from the jump was how few men there were around. I guess I had assumed that my denial was unique to me and that, once it broke, I would enter a community of dads who were doing exactly what I was trying to do. But after a while, I got so used to being the only dad around that I was startled when I saw another father in the hallways. At conferences for parents, usually about 80 percent of the attendees are female.

Where did all the men go?

Now that I've been speaking about autism and getting to know more fathers of special needs children, I have a better sense of what it is about this problem that scares men away. I've also come to realize how important it is for their children and for the fathers themselves that they remain engaged.

After their children are diagnosed, some dads just shut down for a few years. For many, their work life goes to hell too. It's not that they can't deal with their child's autism. It's that they can't deal with themselves.

In the beginning, many fathers see their child's diagnosis as their personal failure. *If there's something wrong with my child, I am less of a man.*

They begin to withdraw from the birthday parties and the picnics that they used to muscle through before the diagnosis gave them a label to describe their child's behavior. Most guys won't admit it because it sounds cruel to say it, but they are ashamed.

"When I looked at all my guy friends who have typical kids, I felt like I had been kicked out of the regular family club," said Erik Linthorst, the director of a documentary about his son, Graham, called *Autistic-Like: Graham's Story.* "I think that this is a cultural thing. The idea that you have to present your family in a certain way to the world: a perfect number of kids, perfect type of activities, perfect wife. I thought I had that, and then the diagnosis took it away."

His mind became filled with anxieties and dire scenarios for the future. "My fantasies of him going to college, getting married, having a family, and being better at all the things that I wish I was better at, were replaced with this bleak outlook of a kid with a severe disorder being around every day for the rest of my life. Being depressed doesn't make you very social. I didn't want to face that world. I wasn't ready."

On the other hand, his wife, Jennie, immediately started seeking out other moms of children on the spectrum. She joined a mom's group and began pulling in a network of support. Suddenly, her friends were bringing over casseroles, and one of them encouraged all of the family's friends to go to an autism fund-raising walk. Jennie urged Erik to find his own guy group to help him cope. She even found some other fathers who were willing to sit down and talk about it with him, but Erik wouldn't do that either. "Call some dude I don't know who wants to have a beer? It breaks the guy code. Never reach out to another dad you don't know for help."

Francisco Fernandez, who is a member of a dad's support group that he found through the L.A.-based organization Autism Speaks, understands what Erik is describing. "We try to recruit dads every year. They come for a while, drop out, and don't return. They won't accept it. They feel that it was something that they did that caused this in their children. We talk about all that in the group. It's not about you, and it's not your fault."

As I know from my own experience, processing your child's diagnosis can sometimes take months, or even years. When I asked Holly what one piece of advice she had for women who were frustrated by their men at this stage, she said, "You have got to cut these guys some slack. You cannot be on him so much and make him feel guilty. He's doing what he thinks he can do, and he must go through it in his own time. My middle name is impatience, and we were in a crisis, but he can't process this any faster than he can process this. That's just how it is."

Once that denial breaks, though, a guy needs a way back into the game.

The special education world is run mostly by women, and a woman's touch is clear in many of the ways the institutions and interactions are organized. Some dads can feel uncomfortable trying to wedge their way into that scene. The first time I tried floor-time with R.J. at Smart Start, I quickly saw that it depended on a patience and tolerance for repetition that did not come naturally to me. I knew it would take me a while to get it right, which meant that there were going to be meltdowns up ahead for R.J. "Dads are not always the most selfless," said Mike Fields, a Tennessee counselor who is the father of a child with autism. "The voice in his head is saying, 'What am I going to get out of this? The kid is not paying attention to me. This is not fun for me.' True, but that can change. You can change that."

My friend Phillip Hain, the executive director of the Los Angeles chapter of Autism Speaks, sums it up well. "It's as simple as the fact that you were thrown this curve in life and that's too bad, but you have to deal with it. Overcome it, or let it overtake you. It's not what you expected and it's not fun, but it is what it is. Who do you want to win? Or, another way of asking the question is, Do you want to be the loser?"

Do you want to be the loser? What man would say yes to that? Yet by stepping away from the family, men lose big-time. They lose their position in the world, the love of their child, and a unique chance to make a difference in the lives of the people that matter to them.

The way men can step back into the game is to focus on the special connection they share with their child. What is your favorite thing to do with your kid? What makes your kid smile and makes you smile? Don't worry about what you have to teach your child, or the goals of your child's therapies. As Mike said, "When you ask the parent of a typical child what they see in their child's future, they don't say they want him to be doctor or a lawyer. They say, 'I want him to be happy.' We get so worried that we tend to forget about joy. We tend to focus too quickly on the superficial—making the kid look normal. We don't want him to stand out or look weird. The problem is not whether or not he's weird. The problem is good weird."

I made my biggest contribution to R.J. through the athletics we practiced at the park, a place where many dads can connect to their children. Much of the work he did in his therapies focused on fine motor skills, like holding the pencil. In the park, we had fun. Fun! Fun is therapeutic too. We made bigger motions—using what they call gross motor skills. We got silly, goofy, childish. I offered him a whole different kind of play.

I know I risk stereotyping the sexes by saying that this is guy stuff. I know some women who would happily and naturally play this way with their sons, just as I've met men who don't know which end of a hammer to hold. Generally speaking, there are some skills and tasks that men gravitate toward teaching their children. But what dads have to offer is more than just the physical.

"There are strengths and capacities in my son that my wife will not be able to bring out," observed Mark Woodsmall, a Los Angeles lawyer whose son is on the spectrum. "I teach him to be a man, and she soothes his wounds. Dad is a little tougher than Mom. Mom is the nurturer, and I have expectations that are pretty high. He adapts his performance based on whom he is working with. She might focus on teaching him how to make friends, but I show him how to handle it when someone rebuffs you. Both those things are relevant."

Seeing the obstacles his son faced and the way the school system supported (and didn't support) families, Mark changed his professional life too. His law practice now focuses exclusively on cases that concern parents' rights under the Individuals with Disabilities Act.

Francisco has a "guy day" with his twelve-year-old son, Miguel, once a week, a day when there are no girls allowed. "There are certain things that he will only discuss with me, and only when we are alone." They go to the movies or to the mall. Francisco feels that the difference between what he offers Miguel and what his wife offers is that Francisco is a little tougher on Miguel. "I never baby him. If he falls and he isn't hurt, I say get up. I don't run right over. I want him to be independent as much as possible."

If Miguel wants ice cream on their "guy day," Francisco doesn't take his order and bring it to him. He makes Miguel buy it himself, even if doing so takes a half an hour. "Whenever he wants something, he has to go find out how much it is," Francisco said. "He goes into the store to see how much a scoop costs and what flavors he wants. Then he comes back to tell me. A dollar a scoop and you can get it in a cup or in a cone. I hand him the money and tell him I want it in a cup and two scoops. He can get whatever he wants too. When he comes back, we count to see if he has the correct change."

Back when they started this routine a few years earlier, Miguel had trouble looking people in the eye and speaking loudly enough to be heard in a shop. This is no longer a problem.

Erik suggests that once you've dropped that initial resistance to the diagnosis and started really engaging with your child, you might want to revisit the idea of joining a men's support group. He did, although the one he attended wasn't just for dads of children on the spectrum, but for dads whose children had a range of disabilities. "These were four guys I could relate to. One man's child has Down's syndrome, another's had cerebral palsy. We could talk like I'd never talked to men before. I knew then that my family's social circle would change, and that was a step in the right direction. The benefit for me was a sense that this was no longer an awful situation that would quarantine my family from the rest of the world. People I admired were also going through it."

Francisco's group meets once a month at a restaurant and has a group outing with their kids a few times a year. When they get together for dinner, they check in on how their children are doing and find out what each of them has been struggling with. They exchange advice on how to talk to others about their children's behavior in public. Many times they talk about money or struggles with getting their parents and relatives to understand their child's condition.

This group has become very important to Francisco, a brotherhood of sorts. He says it has helped him keep his dreams for Miguel alive, while still accepting the reality of what Miguel is today. "Only you know what your child needs," he said. The group has helped him see that. "You are the best advocate for your child. The sooner you realize that and the more active you are in getting him the help he needs, the better your relationship will be."

You're only alone if you choose to be, and that choice is not good for you or your child.

Do you remember when you first held that child in your hands moments after that baby entered the world? I don't know how you felt then, but one of the big things I felt was that suddenly my life wasn't about just me anymore. When we got the diagnosis and I had come through my denial, I understood that I had just been fooling myself when I thought that in the delivery room. I still wanted it all to be about me, and the perfect family portrait I imagined presenting to the world. As long as I had my nightly scotch and cigar, autism wasn't going affect our lives. I could hold on to all the dreams I had when I first held him. It was only when I got myself out of that comfy leather chair and started to understand our real situation that I also understood that life had handed me an incredible opportunity.

My dreams didn't have to die.

In fact, they are bigger and more powerful than anything I could have imagined before.

I had to let go of a lot in order to grab on to the reality of my child and of his world. I'm saying this as a man who has been humbled by the raising of his children. And through that humility, I've become a better father. I stand in the world as a better man with a bigger heart and much more to give, and a much better sense of myself than a scotch and a Monte ever gave me. I was, in Phillip Hain's phrase, very much not the loser in this battle. I gained so much from what R.J. taught me about pride and patience and the limitless nature of the true love between a father and a son. Before my journey with R.J., I now realize, I had a very narrow view of what I wanted for him and what I wanted for my family. Because I took this path with him, I know that his possibilities are wide open, and I feel that he's taught me how to make my heart wide open too.

AFTERWORD

Spring break always finds our family in a tropical place. All of us, and especially R.J., love the water. Last year we rented a beautiful eight-bedroom villa on the sand in Cabo San Lucas that was big enough for everyone in the extended family to enjoy a week away.

I sat in a roomy rattan chair on the balcony of our master suite, watching the kids running through the surf. The weather had been perfect that day, and the sun was setting across a beautiful stretch of pure blue sea. Wisps of thin clouds framed the last shred of the sun, which had just dipped below the horizon, tinting the edges of the sky coral pink.

I listened to the sound of my kids and their cousins, who still had lots of energy even after a morning on the Jet Skis and an afternoon of body surfing. R.J. and Robinson tossed the Frisbee around while Ryan and Roman danced at the edges of the surf. All of us were getting a little restless for dinner. We had reservations at a great fish place in town in about an hour, but I knew we would have liked it to be a little sooner.

This vacation scene would have been unimaginable to us six years ago when we stayed at the Grand Wailea on Maui for spring break. On that vacation, even the simple act of going to a restaurant was a nightmare for us. Not only would R.J. only eat a few things—French fries, pasta, and maybe pizza—but on that trip he also had the meltdown of meltdowns.

Our first night there we all went to dinner and R.J. screamed and cried and wouldn't eat anything. He yelled at the waiters and refused to sit for more than five minutes at a time. Holly and I took turns walking with him to try to calm him down. We felt as though the whole dining room was glaring at us. Our family had ruined everyone's dinner. After that, we never went to another restaurant on Maui. We were there for eight days and we ordered room service for seven of them.

Our anxiety stretched to the grounds outside our room. The hotel has great water slides and is very kid friendly. They have plenty of lifeguards, and families feel safe enough to let their kids roam the property alone and seek out their own fun, but not my boy. R.J. was a good swimmer, but he was a daredevil. He also didn't quite understand the concept of checking in every twenty minutes. Even with help and the multiple lifeguards, I didn't want to let him out of my sight.

What a world of difference Cabo was when compared to that disaster of a trip to Hawaii. R.J. participated in every activity and played easily with his brothers, sister, and cousins. He even ate everything that was put on his plate. One day, we went fishing and caught a couple of mahimahi. R.J. named one Pierre. Later that night we had Pierre for dinner and R.J. ate every bite. Five years earlier, he wouldn't eat fish. He wouldn't ride on a Jet Ski.

Mexico last spring was the most relaxing family vacation I've ever had. I could feel it as I sat on the balcony with Holly at my side, more beautiful to me than the day we were married. We'd been through so much. The day she shouted me out of denial. The fact that she didn't leave me. How we stood together and told the world how precious our son was. Holly and I always considered ourselves the perfect teammates. For a short while our team had been out of sync. But R.J. had helped Holly and me remember why we love each other. He taught us to work together and trust each other again. R.J. helped us understand what Team Peete was all about, and sitting on that balcony in Mexico, I realized we were *all* on board.

In Cabo I sat on the balcony instead of hiding out in a cigar lounge. And thought that there was nothing better than watching my whole family play in the pool, on the beach, with one another.

It was the vacation I had always wanted, with the family I had always dreamed of.

THE WELCOME TO AUTISM HANDBOOK

INTRODUCTION

When my son R.J. was first diagnosed as being on the autistic spectrum, Holly and I sat in the doctor's office stunned, unable to do anything except hold each other's hands. In the weeks that followed, we wished there had been some guidebook that the doctor could have handed to us that explained what we should do next.

As you know from reading this book, we believed that the doctor who diagnosed R.J. didn't give us enough information to decide what our next step would be. As I worked on this book, I decided that if there wasn't a "Welcome to Autism Handbook," I could at least steer readers to some of the places that could help them start making a plan of action.

First thing, before we get into specifics, I'm going to offer a few general observations:

1) Don't panic, it is not the end of the world. But first you must

put away your pride and ego. What you might have thought of as the way to raise your child has now suddenly changed.

2) There are many resources out there and a wealth of information. There have been many advances in the eight years since we began our journey.

3) Speak frankly with your pediatrician. Don't be afraid to ask questions. Remember the old cliché, "There is no such thing as a dumb question." Make sure he or she answers all of your questions and concerns. And if he or she can't, tell him or her to find someone who can. Raising children is not an exact science and neither is the treatment of a child on the spectrum. Your pediatrician must be open to new or different ideas. Trust your gut and that parental intuition.

4) Talk, talk, talk. Time is vital, so there is NO time for self-pity, stubbornness, or, as in my case, denial. Remember, it is not about you, it is about your child, so the quicker you get on board, the better it will be for your child. Talk to your spouse, significant other, brothers, sisters, and all family members and close friends. Creating a team around your child is so important in the early years. It can be an exhausting journey, and having a strong support system will take some of the stress and pressure off of you. In our case some friends and family had to take a backseat because they weren't on board with our program.

5) Educate yourself and your team on how to interact with your child. A child on the spectrum can be intimidating to an adult or another child if you are not informed on how to speak, play, or work with a child with autism. I had my wake-up call during a session of floortime, and thank God I did, because prior to it, I had not been helping R.J.'s therapy.

6) Test for allergies. And if you did it before your diagnosis, do it again. Allergies can have dramatic effects on kids with autism. R.J. was allergic to wheat gluten and once we got him off that we saw positive changes in him.

7) Diet! Speak with your doctor and a nutritionist together. The healthier the diet, the better R.J. focused, in school and in therapy sessions.

8) Sleep. Make sure your child is getting plenty of rest.

9) Be open to alternative therapies. I refer back to #4, talk, because you can't talk enough to other families—and compare notes. You will be amazed how many families with a child on the spectrum are willing to share what works for them. Always consult with your doctor before you try something new.

I hope you find what we offer here to be useful as a guide to some of the things you should consider. I am not a doctor, and this is not medical or legal advice. Instead, what I want to give you here is a pathway to explore—suggestions about things you should take a look at, as well as some of the things we did as we walked along that same path. Remember, though, every child on the spectrum presents unique talents and deficiencies. No one family's response to it looks like another's. These are some general areas to consider as you and your family decide how you will begin to face this challenge.

GENERAL RESOURCES

http://www.autismspeaks.org/

Founded by the grandparents of an autistic child, this site provides a host of information on autism. They are also advocates for autism awareness, having started chapters of Autism Speaks around the globe. On this site you can download Autism Speaks' "100 Day Kit," a useful step-by-step handbook that can take you through the first one hundred days starting from diagnosis.

http://www.autismsource.org/

A huge national database of autism-related resources and support services. This Autism Society Web site can be searched regionally or by individual topics.

http://www.autismweb.com/

A parent's guide to autism, offering general information on the spectrum, a large list of autism-related books, a calendar of events related to autism, and a cyber parental-support group.

*Autism Spectrum Disorders from A to Z: Assessment, Diagnosis . . . &
More!* by Barbara T. Doyle and Emily Doyle Iland. Pegasus Books,
2008.

Very detailed step-by-step volume covering symptoms, defi-
nitions, assessments, diagnoses, and more. Written in plain language, this book is a useful resource for those faced with a new
diagnosis.

A Regular Guy: Growing Up With Autism by Laura Shumaker.
Landscape Press, 2008.

An inspiring chronicle by the mother of an autistic child, this
story follows her son Matthew from diagnosis at age two into his
twenties.

http://www.woodbinehouse.com/

Woodbine House is a publisher specializing in books about
children with special needs. They have a huge collection of
books and other media on autism and celiac disease.

DIET

http://www.gfcfdiet.com/

http://www.celiacsociety.org/

*Eating for Autism: The 10-Step Nutrition Plan to Help Treat Your
Child's Autism, Asperger's, or ADHD* by Elizabeth Strickland, MS,
RD, LD. DaCapo Press, 2009.

A comprehensive volume on diet strategies, with detailed information on allergy testing, interpreting allergy tests, vitamin therapies, and nutritional detox. Provides sources for purchasing casein, gluten, and additive-free products.

The Autism & ADHD Diet: A Step-by-Step Guide to Hope and Healing by Living Gluten Free and Casein Free (GFCF) and Other Interventions by Barrie Silberberg. Sourcebooks Inc., 2009.

Written by the parent of an autistic child, this book offers a personal perspective on how to maintain a GFCF diet. Includes menus, label-reading guides, strategies for eating out, and stories from other families who found the diet helpful.

Son Rise: The Miracle Continues by Barry Neil Kaufman and Raun Kaufman. H.J. Kramer, 1995.

A passionate book about parents whose intensive homemade floortime therapy dramatically helped their son. Inspiring and emotional, with a message that helps you not give up hope.

COMPLEMENTARY THERAPIES AND LEARNING TOOLS

Engaging Autism: Helping Children Relate, Communicate, and Think with the DIR Floortime Approach by Stanley I. Greenspan, MD, and Serena Wieder, PhD. DaCapo Press, 2006.

This volume explains the DIR/Floortime Model of playing

with an autistic child in order to teach social interaction and communication skills.

http://www.icdl.com

The Web site for the Interdisciplinary Council on Developmental and Learning Disorders (ICDL), founded by Stanley Greenspan, MD, developer of the DIR/Floortime Model. The site provides links to DIR professionals and school programs that utilize the DIR method.

Understanding Sensory Dysfunction: Learning, Development and Sensory Dysfunction in Autism Spectrum Disorders, ADHD, Learning Disabilities and Bipolar Disorder, by Polly Godwin Emmons and Liz McKendry Anderson. Jessica Kingsley Publishers, 2004.

A detailed overview of contributing factors and behaviors associated with sensory dysfunction as it occurs in autism spectrum disorders, ADHD, and bipolar disorder. Includes assessment and curricular tools and integration activities for parents and teachers.

Helping Children with Autism Learn: Treatment Approaches for Parents and Professionals, by Bryna Siegel, PhD. Oxford University Press, 2003.

Identifying the myriad challenges children on the spectrum can face, this book offers dedicated chapters on specific learning differences, providing a guide for development of the best education plan for the individual learner.

Overcoming Autism: Finding the Answers, Strategies, and Hope That Can Transform a Child's Life, by Lynn Kern Koegel, PhD, and Claire LaZebnik. Penguin Books, 2004.

A practical resource describing behavioral teaching methods and strategies for developing social skills in the ASD Child.

DVDs

Autism: The Musical (2007)

Starring: Elaine Hall and Rosanne Katon. A documentary about how Elaine's inventive way of dealing with autistic children allows them to blossom through a theater performance.

Autistic-Like: Graham's Story (2009)

Director: Erik Linthorst

This is an intimate family portrait showing one dad's determined quest to find the right therapies, the right doctors, and even the right words to describe his son.